Kim —
thank you,
Pam

Bluebird Publishing Co.
PO Box 4538
St. Louis, MO 63108
www.bluebirdbookpub.com

S.O.S. From Suburbia

Secrets of Juggling Parenthood, Chocolate...and Fun

Pam Wilson

For Joe and Jessie...
Defy Gravity

Acknowledgements

Thank you to all the early readers who gave such positive encouragement and provided many, many topics to write about. This wouldn't be complete without thanking all of my girlfriends who continually read whatever I write and for all of those friends who need to be reminded to read (even Carrie Bradshaw's friends didn't always read everything she wrote!). A special thanks to Jenny Wolkowitz who helped me edit, re-write and bounce ideas around. I appreciate all of the hard work of Carol Holden, my illustrator who brought the book to life with her drawings and Sharon Greenstein for her amazing ideas which we used. I wish I looked like the character we came up with! Thanks to the great people at Bluebird: Dan Thompson, Jeff Fister and a big hurrah for Jennifer Fandel who held my hand throughout this process. Jennifer, I still owe you a chocolate martini. Rachel Otto, wherever you are-thank you for taking a chance on me all those years ago with my idea about writing about my life here in suburbia. For all of the Savvy Family (now St. Louis Moms and Dads) professionals who help me sound great every month and all the readers who read every month-thank you!!! For all the listening, encouragement and chocolate I thank my sister Staci Pruitt who is the nicest person I know. Thanks to Fran Levy for the editing and Gary Zenk, photographer extraordinaire who made me feel and look like a rock star. Thanks to my fellow TOM's: Laura Ray and Ellie Grossman who shared information, contacts and writing advice-wow. Can you believe it? This effort is also for my Uncle Steve who famously said to me, "Keep writing," on one of our last visits. I have and I will. Lastly (although always first in my eyes, heart and life) my heart-felt gratitude to "those people who live in my house" and make my life crazy, chaotic and so worth every stretch mark and gray hair: Kenny, Joe and Jessie-without you life would not be as exciting or wonderful or worth-while. These are our stories and I appreciate being part of them with you.

Table of Contents

Good Day Sunshine

What I Did For Love

Our House is a Very Fine House

I've Got All My Sisters with Me

Secrets of Surviving:

Good Day Sunshine

S.O.S. From Suburbia

How in the world did I end up here? How does a beach bunny end up in landlocked St. Louis, smack in the middle of suburban life?

This wasn't supposed to be my life. I dreamed of going to New York and writing for magazines, never getting married, and having lots of friends. You know–a fabulous life. In high school, whenever I was asked, this would always be my answer. I would write and explore and travel and have it all.

As luck, fate and the universe would have it; my path did not lead me to New York to write. Somewhere along the way, I realized I would have to be practical and support myself. Though I had written all my life (some really bad stuff), my writing was not a priority to me in college. I see now that I wasn't ready to write. I didn't have much to write about at that time. Even in creative writing classes, my efforts weren't that interesting.

Enter real life.

When I finally found myself in the school where I thrived, I was working with young children and their families. I was good at it and enjoyed it, although I could barely pay my bills. Heading back to graduate school, I managed to do some writing, but still nothing of much interest.

Then a funny thing happened. I found a life.

I ended up earning a Masters of Social Work degree, getting married and then having kids.

And *that's* how I ended up in suburbia. At the ripe old age of 40, I took a look around and realized that there had to be something more.

There was.

When an injury sidelined me, forcing me to be still (not one of my favorite things), I began to write. I wrote about what I knew, which was raising a family and living here in suburbia. I still write what I know and now I realize I know what I write.

But I knew that the nuts and bolts of day to day life aren't all that interesting, so I kept writing until I was able to find my voice. As I was doing that, I realized that I was emphasizing the humor in everyday aspects of life. By sharing what I was living and struggling with, I found that readers were identifying with the stories and finding comfort in the knowledge that we are not alone. The same things are happening in all our households. It's how we deal with them that defines and ultimately shapes who we and our families are.

I wrote about the lunacy of raising kids in today's world: crazy sports coaches, even crazier moms living through their daughters, pole dancing, struggling to make dinner each night, the absence of sleep, strong women helping one another, the glory of a pedicure, raising a teenage boy, taming curly hair, the love of chocolate and allowing ice cream for dinner. It was all funny and clever in my head.

I figured out a way to get it on paper and then I started telling people about it. My friend Eric gifted me with the best description of my writing: "It's like 'Sex and the City' without the sex and without the city." That story has been told…really well in books, TV and movies. This, my story is a different story. This is the story of life here in suburbia in the middle of the country. While it would be nice to live like Carrie Bradshaw in the city… I wonder how Carrie would fare here in suburbia. Running to the grocery store in five inch heels does get a little trying.

It's my life and all the craziness of a beach girl surviving suburbia while raising responsible, interesting kids, getting dinner on the table, running car-pool and dancing with my girlfriends.

The journey that started over twenty years ago continues. I realized fairly late in the game that the universe knew exactly what I needed the whole time. With a few little spins (how far is the beach?) I knew I could make suburbia survivable, and I have!

"S.O.S. from Suburbia" is a universal story. We all have strategies to survive. It might be amazing girlfriends, reading books, or that comfortable couch that is so welcoming each night. The point is to juggle everything and find a balance we can live with. I do it every day, and I'll bet you do, too. Survival doesn't have to have a negative connotation-in fact, survival strategies and how we make it work is quite positive. For me, it's living every day and finding all the good stuff that makes life worthwhile. Like dancing. Chocolate. Sunshine. Like those little faces that come home after school every day smiling because we are here. Like the good night hug of a 14 year old-man-boy.

I often wonder if all of these survival strategies are causing me to lose my mind OR if all of these amazing components of suburbia are actually my secrets of surviving with great hair, margaritas and good friends. More than anything, I hope that these stories inspire you, whether you are a new mom, a veteran mom, or somewhere in between. I hope you can relate to the craziness of it all. Because while it is crazy and messy and loud, it is real life. It is suburbia at its best.

Pretty Feet and Toes

I have great feet. I really do. I'm not ashamed to tell you so. I have great feet and toes. By the way, they are amazing in sandals.

They are a part of my body that I've always known were great. I can't work out to improve them. I've accepted them as I have never accepted my thighs. My feet never lost their perkiness from nursing babies. My feet never had to endure thousands of crunches to become flatter after I gave birth.

In time, I made my peace with my less than perky breasts. They had, after all, nursed two children. My tummy and I had called a truce. It didn't look like it did when I was 25, but at least it was respectably firm. My thighs, well, my thighs and I agreed to disagree as long as there are brownies in the world. My feet, however—well, my feet are great. Slender and long, with toes that are the correct lengths in varying degrees. For some unknown reason, they always look tan and I always paint my toenails bright pink or purple.

It wasn't until I was 40 and my dad found out I had never had a manicure or pedicure that I discovered the pleasure and seduction of pedicures. Dad told me it would be his treat: the works. I gathered information and asked friends for suggestions. After all, this first time needed to be as close to heaven as possible. Friends recommended a spa-like atmosphere for my first pedicure.

I loved it. And hated it.

I found out that I wasn't exactly a manicure person. However, I immediately fell in love with the pedicure. I loved what my feet felt like and what they looked like. I just had to find the right place.

I tried a number of places. Through word of mouth and gifts, I have been to really expensive places and the tech places as well. My most indulgent pedicure treatment to date was at Heartland Spa outside Chicago. However I have found places right here in St. Louis that I worship.

Of all the services that I classify as indulgent, I will make an exception for pedicures and facials. Last year for Mother's Day, I told my children to please get me chocolate from Bissinger's, perfume and a pedicure. I've done this every holiday since, and I'm here to tell you, my feet have been well taken care of this year.

Here's the flip side of indulgence for a mom. I always think, "Oh, this $35 could pay for a pair of jeans for the kids or a pair of shoes, or an art class for someone." It would even pay for babysitting Saturday night.

I am not extravagant. I love Old Navy jeans. I live in yoga pants and tennis shoes. But the thought of taking care of me, just me, sometimes goes beyond what I can do. It's a mother's job to take care of everyone else. Why is it so hard for moms to take care of themselves? Why don't we allow ourselves to do this?

I shoo the guilt away. If I take care of me, I can take care of everyone else in a renewed state of mind. I will allow myself the time and expense. In my world, it makes me a better mom.

The luxury and pure decadence of a pedicure gently enfolds me and coaxes me to forget the grocery store, the cleaning and the next errand. The peace that a pedicure offers is worth $35.

All it takes is 45 minutes. Forty-five minutes to rejuvenate my feet and therefore my soul. Not to mention the added bonus of great looking toes.

I often think I could be at softball practice, playing catch or reading a book with one of my kids. I have an endless list of errands and household chores. I push all those thoughts out of my mind and relax as my feet and legs are smoothed. Everything is tingling. When I am finished, I sigh in complete bliss. I have brought my favorite Cinnamon Girl flip-flops; purple flowers adorn the edges. I look at my feet. They are even lovelier. They are smoothed and silky. They are, quite simply, great feet.

I feel like a new person. No amount of crossing off on the to-do list makes me feel this way. I am ready to play catch, read books, and return to my life. I have happy feet....my soul rejoices.

Supermom

"Mom, can you make me another waffle?" Joe asked this morning. I looked at him, then at the toaster oven, and I couldn't even muster the energy or enthusiasm for breakfast. I sighed.

It wasn't even that big of a request; it was just that my list is way too long. I have overextended myself and I can't see straight. Add to that a sinus infection that I am trying to treat with Dayquil because I don't have the energy to call the doctor; physical therapy three times a week for an ankle injury; agreeing to serve pie at the fifth-grade Harvest Festival this Friday; and the desperate need of Valerie to color the gray right out of my hair.

In short, I am just like every other mom (and dad) around here. Overextended, busy, crazy, short-tempered, and craving chocolate.

So, this morning, when Kenny asked me why I was so crabby, I had to stop and think. It's just too much. All of it. The laundry, a healthy dinner every night, keeping up with this house, the kids, carpools, housework, friends. How do other people do it?

As Joe was walking out of the house this morning I said, "I'm going to try to not be so crabby anymore," to which this very smart 10-year-old answered, "That's a good thing to work on."

When I got to the park where I was meeting Jenny for a much-needed bike ride in this unseasonably warm November weather, she said, "I have too many balls in the air!"

"Join the club!" I smiled.

"Okay, you tell me your list and then I'll tell you mine," she offered.

"If I have to empty the dishwasher one more time, I am going to scream," I began and we both laughed.

She knew exactly what I meant. It's not just one thing, it's everything. It's all the laundry and the dinners and the phone calls. It's everything that makes this house hum plus all the things I want to actually do that never get done. My to-do list became so detailed and long I had to throw it away. (It scared me to look at it!) My new system (and by the way it works so much better) are tiny yellow Post-its scattered in the top desk drawer.

I knew I had to put an end to the crabbiness quickly. Today. Immediately. Because grumpiness is contagious.

"Between everything that is going on and trying to keep up, I am really overwhelmed," I finally admitted to Kenny by phone. This is hard to admit. I've always believed that I can handle it. I can handle it all. I am…Supermom.

But I'm not.

And if I were, Supermom is one tired woman.

Besides, my cape is in the laundry. (I am envisioning Lynda Carter's Wonder Woman here, but have a feeling I am more like Mrs. Incredible.)

As I have talked more and more to other moms about this, it seems that we all have similar feelings. Overwhelmed, not overjoyed. How did *that* happen?

I remember something my friend Sheri said to me a few years ago. I was telling her my frustration with how life was changing and moving so fast. The only time my kids are still is at night, when they are sleeping. I love to watch them while they sleep. I always have. (I even have pictures of them sleeping.) But lately, it seems that, when I go in to peek, I feel so guilty.

"You feel guilty because you feel blessed and you don't feel like you are enjoying them," Sheri commented.

How am I supposed to enjoy these guys when I am hustling them to finish homework, getting them to baseball practice, and trying my best to get them into showers each night?

When you have kids, isn't it an excuse to be childlike again? To laugh and play and run and jump?

But then, who is in charge?

Supermom, of course.

I have always said, leave the dishes, leave the cleaning, and be with the kids. (But you know I always have excuses for not doing housework.) When they were little, it was so much easier to just hang out and play. As they have gotten older, the demands on my time in many different areas have increased. Yes, they still want me to play catch and basketball; however, the *need* for meals and laundry has not decreased. It feels like it's increased.

Our household needs a super hero!

Here's the thing. I know how lucky we are. If I really am a Supermom (here's the cape thing again), then here is my superpower: the ability to lighten the load of stress and pressure on myself, thereby alleviating stress on the family. So what if we are late once in a while? So what if dinner is a PB&J (on whole wheat)? So what if we continue in our quest to just hang out together as a family as often as possible?

Enjoying and embracing my kids' free-thinking, silly, made-up songs and outrageous plans are my new superpowers. Laughing more, dancing more and living more with my children in the present is the most super gift I can ever give to them and myself.

I am not saying any of this is easy. I am just saying I need to give this particular superpower a try. I feel like time is speeding by. I don't want to miss another minute of the fun or laughter.

Besides, I really like the idea of a cape.

Confessions of a Suburban Drama Queen

When Jessie was still in elementary school, we met friends in the park one day after school. There were old friends and new friends for both of us. One of the women, someone I didn't know well, asked if she could bounce a story off some of us. She then launched into a 25-minute account about something that obviously bothered her a great deal. She looked directly at me and said, "You know this person, so I'm not going to use names." Well of course that got me wondering who it could possibly be.

When it was time to leave, my acquaintance actually divulged whom she was talking about. Never in my wildest dreams would I have guessed. Since there were other people involved in the story, she let me know those names as well. I hadn't expected this but I wasn't shocked. In any case, her story didn't have any particular impact on me.

Apparently, the woman just needed to vent, and a number of us happened to be there to listen. No problem solving was necessary. And even more important, her anecdote had nothing to do with me. I drove away without giving it another thought.

Jessie and I talked about who she played with that day, what we would do the rest of the afternoon (we were having dinner parties at our house both Friday and Saturday) and our weekend plans.

The following Monday there was a voice-mail for me from a friend who, as it happened, had been one of the people named in the story told to me at the park. She was concerned because our mutual acquaintance had informed her that she had related the story to me.

Instead of calling her back, I e-mailed her. It was just easier. I wrote something to the effect that I'd forgotten the whole thing. After all, I wrote, "I have my own drama to deal with." I didn't have time to deal with her drama—I have enough of my own. I'm lucky to get through my own day with all of the drama swirling around me...

I thought of all my own "dramas of the moment": What do we need to do for the third-grade leaf project? Why is Jessie suddenly shy at ballet? Does Joe really need to take guitar lessons along with everything else he is doing? Should we take a trip over winter break? Can I get out of working on this committee? Does the dog need a bath? What's for dinner? Do we have eggs? How did everyone run out of clean socks at the same time? I'd really love to work on a campaign.

And then of course there are friends who are having their own dramas. As your friend, I would love to hear about your drama if you need to share it. If you need me to listen, to cry with you, to go out and celebrate with you (anytime!), I am here, 100%. My friends know this. It is implicit in our relationship.

My friend Cheryl put it best: "When you choose to open yourself to someone, you are choosing to invest yourself in that person." But it is a choice. And honestly? Trust and friendship are a two-way street. I have found that I don't open up easily, but if I do, it's because I really trust you.

In the same vein, I am the most loyal friend you will ever find. I will support you completely because you are my friend. (As long as you're not into dangerous stuff.) I will glory in your triumphs. I am one of the friends yelling, "You go, girl!" I will be there with chocolate when you are sad. I may not be the warmest and fuzziest, but I am the most loyal.

I also ask lots of questions. Of everyone. All the time. I want to hear as many opinions as possible, not because I don't know what to do, but because your insight might help me see something that I was missing because I'm too involved in my own drama. I'm seeing the trees, but not the forest. I need to hear other points of view. Which part of the forest can a friend shed light on? Therefore, I feel I'm a very good listener, too.

Getting back to drama. If you think about it, we are all living with our own dramas. We are living in the worlds which we have created. Our resources are limited. There are only so many hours in the day, and only so many things we can think about. Honestly, I have no time for my own drama…let alone drama that doesn't involve me.

Since e-mailing my friend about her drama, I have noticed many times over the weeks how much drama we all contend with. It's also intriguing to me how people deal with their problems. I am a problem solver. I want to fix everything and quickly. Then move on to happier things.

On the other hand, some people just need to be drama queens, which is also okay. If you're one of them, you should know, though, that other people may not respond the way you want them to–not unless you let give them the opportunity and time to do that. And even then, most people will want to steer clear of the drama.

Sometimes people just want to talk. Sometimes people need your help. Sometimes, like me, people are looking for insight.

So drama-mama's of the world…let's all get out our tiaras at the same time. Together let's put them on. Let's recite our Drama Queen mantra, "Your drama is not my drama!" Somehow some way we will all get through our dramas one at a time. Slowly or quickly, but with the grace, dignity and good humor we bring to each situation. Maybe if we are lucky, our tiaras will still be intact.

Hand over the chocolate and nobody will get hurt.

Hi, my name is Pam and I am a chocoholic.

Not just a normal chocoholic, but a dyed-in-the-M&M-bag chocoholic.

Easily said, not so easy to change. I have to believe it's genetic because my son is as well. We will choose chocolate above all other options, including and not limited to survival on an ongoing basis. And sometimes, yes, I've been known to say, "move away from the chocolate and nobody will get hurt."

When I travel, I am on a quest for three things: local coffee, foods indigenous to the region and chocolate. I have been known to walk a mile out of my way to find some sort of local treat. I read travel and cooking magazines constantly, so if I spot an article about a certain chocolate, it gets filed away until that knowledge can be made useful.

I do not squander my chocolate calories mindlessly, but I am not a chocolate snob. So on some days, peanut butter M&Ms (in the red package) are it, and on other days, nothing but Bissinger's chocolate-covered raisins will do. There have been many nights when chocolate chips are more than adequate. Like all chocoholics, I have a variety of chocolate chips in my pantry at all times.

My weaknesses include (and this order changes by the day, even the hour) ooey-gooey, rich-beyond-belief brownies; soft, warm, just-baked chocolate chip cookies; ice cream and gelato (any variety, but no ice milk please); and chocolate candy. (I have been through many phases and varieties. Anything with peanut butter is pure decadence for me.) Chocolate cannot be in my house. I know my limits. I know myself all too well. If it's here, it relentlessly calls to me and, I have to admit…I have no control!

So here's the latest concern: is all this chocolate healthy for me? Last summer, I tried to go sugar free (a modified version of the South Beach Diet). I have to admit, I felt better. I thought I looked better. I struggled. Everyone in my house was confused by my utter crabbiness on a daily basis.

When my son Joe was 6 months old, I read something written by a sports psychologist. He recommended that his clients reserve a time during each week when they could indulge in their "problem food." (Here I must laugh…because I don't have a problem "food"; I have a problem "food group".) I chose Saturday afternoons. During those first weeks, I would stand at the pantry door in the middle of the week and say, "You can do this. Walk away from the chocolate." And I did. Grudgingly. Slowly. Looking back and knowing it was there.

Those first few Saturdays were chocolate frenzies. It would be only noon and I would be eating something outrageous I had thought about all week. And then something more. It was almost too much for one day. I wasn't even sure if I was eating any less chocolate. It was just contained to one day during the week.

Finally one week, Saturday came and went, and I hadn't thought about chocolate at all. And I wasn't craving it either. I couldn't believe it. I actually went and survived an entire week without chocolate.

Impossible.

However, just so we're staying on the up and up here…that chocolate-free week happened only that one time. By the next week, I was back to dreaming in chocolate.

Currently I am thinking about health. I exercise to be strong and healthy (okay, I admit for a flat stomach, too!) To be strong and healthy, nutritionally, it would make sense to follow a sensible eating plan: lots of fruits and veggies and forgo the chocolate.

Sigh.

Why does that sound so boring? Where is the chocolate? Where is the excitement? My friend Patti, who is one of the most well-balanced persons I know, countered with a huge "WHY?" when I mentioned one afternoon that I might give up chocolate. She has a point.

Life is so short. I eat vegetables and fruit, wheat germ and flax seed, so by the laws of compensatory eating, it all balances itself out! In my world, chocolate *is* a food group.

So here I am, once more struggling with my chocolate consumption. I have found that I have a tremendous tolerance for chocolate. Case in point: my sister has learned to make candy. Her first attempt at peppermint patties was a delicious dozen for me. (A dozen in a two-day span!) I have no stopping point. I have no control. I have to talk to Oprah.

I pleaded with my sister, "No matter *what* I say, do *not* give me any more of these!" So far, she has kept her promise. I wonder whom it's harder on, her or me? I've only asked her for a supply once; she laughed and gave me a firm *no!*

Once again I am questioning my relationship with chocolate. Why must I have it? Why do I crave it? And more important, *how can I make peace with chocolate?* You know, I really just want my jeans to fit. Some days I can completely forgo chocolate. And other days…if I don't have my "fix," I just know someone better hand over that chocolate and nobody will get hurt.

We Got the Beat!

I am singing at the top of my lungs and dancing so hard and fast I am sure I am going to fly out of my dancing boots. I haven't stopped smiling since The Go-Gos hit the stage, belting out "Vacation" and the happiness hasn't stopped.

I can't believe I am here with these rocker chicks, who look and sound better than ever. My sister (who graciously said "yes" when I called and said, "I have a huge favor to ask…") is rocking out beside me. We are laughing and screaming and jumping up and down in the fourth row for the very warm, very personable Go-Gos. These chicks look like every other mom in suburbia. But they're The Go-Gos!

It almost didn't happen. The Go-Gos show sold out quicker than I could get a ticket. I simply wasn't taking no for an answer. After I exchanged e-mails with Scott at Ameristar, he quickly became my hero by understanding my *need* to be at the show. Somehow, Scott managed to find two extra tickets, and the excitement began to build. Upon meeting Scott, I threw my arms around him as he looked at my sister and asked, "Is she always like this?" When we are talking The Go-Gos, David Cassidy, Daniel Day-Lewis or the Bradys… ummm, yes!

While the Go-Gos *look* like every other mom we might know, they are members of the very first "girl band." They defined the sound, the look and the feel for generations of girls who felt the need to rock and roll. They are the group that spoke to us when we were in college and trying to make sense of boys who didn't make sense. They are still speaking to us now, almost thirty years later. They sound *better than ever.*

And they have a lot to say.

You know those moments in your life that you will always remember: earning an A in a challenging college course, getting the job you wanted, having a child. Well, the *moment* that Gina hit those drums and the Go-Gos came out dancing to "Vacation" is something I will always remember. It was like watching freedom dance across the stage. Another life, another time, another self.

"I want to be a Go-Go," I commented to my friend Patti two days later. It didn't matter which one. I could sing, dance, play the drums, whatever was needed.

"In another life, I think," she answered, not missing a beat. (smile)

No, I think to myself as I drive around suburbia doing errands for my family. No, I want to be a Go-Go *now*. I want to rock out. I want to be the talent and inspiration to thousands of girls everywhere. I want to follow a dream, smile slyly and remind the world that "Our lips are sealed." I want to have the hand-eye coordination to play the drums like Gina and rock the guitar like Jane and Kathy and Charlotte. I want to sing like Belinda. I want–I *need* to be a Go-Go. (Or at the very least, a back-up singer.)

Just tell me what I have to do.

For the past two days I have been listening nonstop to my Go-Gos CD. My family has continually asked me to "please turn it down." Until they finally give up and sing along with me. Every time a song comes on that the Go-Gos sang Thursday night, I have visions of those girls on the stage, playing guitar. Imagine, if you will, four girls lined up across the stage, singing, dancing and laughing and letting us know they are still "Mad About You." I can feel myself letting go, dancing and laughing and getting a glimpse of the girl that was.

Oh, my inner rocker-chick needs to get out more!

I still have so many dreams besides rocking out on stage. I still want to write the great American novel, dance on Broadway and somehow make a difference in the world. Dancing and singing with The Go-Go's made me remember that fun girl. From now on, I am letting my inner rocker chick shine upon suburbia. We'll see how she does. She's still here…Oh yea, I know she is. "We got the beat! Everybody, get on your feet!."

Once Upon a Mattress

Once upon a time, there lived a lovely maiden who was tired all of the time. Not just your usual-I-have-two-kids-and-a-house-to-take-care-of-tired, but real, bone-deep exhaustion. She didn't understand why she was so tired all the time. She slept every night and woke either with the dog or the sun. Yet, our fair maiden was indeed very, very tired.

For she was a maiden who really liked her sleep. Not only did she like her sleep, she needed her sleep to be able to function like a human being. Without her sleep, she was cranky and crabby (and needed more chocolate than usual). The fair maiden was certain that she was getting enough sleep, but almost every morning, she awoke exhausted.

One day, she was talking with her doctor, and her doctor asked, "Are you actually sleeping at night?" Hmmm, thought the fair maiden, "I think I am." But that night after she went to bed, she tried very hard to pay attention to whether she slept or not.

(I know, really hard to do.)

It turns out that our fair maiden was actually being awakened during the night–no, not by a pea under the mattress (but good guess!), but by her knight in shining armor, who was not sleeping *at all*. He tossed and turned and twitched, and woke up our fair maiden three or four times every night. He never woke up, of course. What made this even worse was that our fair maiden was sleeping on an old-time, free-flow waterbed (the kind without baffles...from the 70s).

Now, while this might sound interesting, it actually was...annoying. Because the bed had no baffles, every time the knight tossed about or moved at all, not only was the fair maiden woken up, but she had a very hard time getting back to sleep. Every night. For years. There was a lot of chocolate being eaten during the daytime.

The fair maiden decided that they needed a new bed. A real bed. One that didn't involve water. For while that was an interesting conversation starter (and fun for the kids to jump on) our fair maiden was completely exhausted. If they found a new bed, one that was comfortable for both of them, maybe then she wouldn't wake up when the knight tossed and turned.

Alas, the knight liked the waterbed and didn't want to trade it in.

So, the fair maiden tried her best to sleep on the water bed, but when she was awakened in the middle of the night, she wound up on the couch or the extra bed. She was getting more and more frustrated and began dragging the knight to furniture stores to check out modern beds that didn't need water.

It took almost two years for the knight to even agree to try a new bed. Our fair maiden was incredibly tired!

The first bed they tried was too soft.

So they returned it.

The second bed they tried was too hard.

So they returned that one, too.

Their thirty days of trying out mattresses was nearing an end, when the knight, now desperate for a good night's sleep as well, found what he thought was a bed that was…

Just right.

No kidding. It really happened that way.

It's been a year now, and the fair maiden has been sleeping through the night. What a difference it makes to wake up fully rested and ready to take on any fire-breathing dragon that might come along. The knight still tosses and turns and twitches most nights, but the fair maiden, on her side of the just-right bed, just sleeps peacefully through it.

The End.

The Boss of Me

"You're not the boss of me!" one of my kids grumbled.

"Oh, yes I *am!* I am the Boss!" I replied.

Come on, do I really *want* to be the boss of anybody? I can't even control my hair, how can I expect to be the boss of anybody else?!

The answer simply is *no*.

I do *not* want to be the Boss of anybody. Most days that includes me.

I am, however, in charge. I am in charge of this family and everything that comes along with it. How in the world did this happen to a happy-go-lucky surfer girl who just wanted to save the world?!!!

Where did I go wrong? When did I make the detour into being a grown-up and being responsible for other people?

Many years ago when I was selected for a leadership group, at the very first meeting the facilitator had thrown crayons out all over the table. "Choose what color you are," she directed.

Purple and green. I am both. With a little pink thrown in.

We then went around the room and introduced ourselves with our crayons. I only remember one other person's response, my friend Tami. She chose the black crayon, and when it was her turn she said, "I am the black line in my family. Everyone else comes off or through the black line, which runs straight down the center."

As I got to know Tami better I understood more clearly why she felt this way. She was the parent of two teenage girls and the step-parent (and half- custodial parent) of an additional two college-age daughters and a high-school son. They were all treated exactly the same, with equal amounts of energy, humor, and thought. I came to admire Tami in many ways, most specifically her parenting abilities and the confidence with which she moved through her world, completely in charge.

I hadn't thought about this discussion or the black crayon in many years. And then lately as my kids got older, I began to see how someone, anyone, in a family or household *needed* to be the consistent-calm-always-there-always-available-to-talk-or-drive-somewhere adult.

Seriously.

If the universe really knew me, would I be the one in charge of the environment for a husband, two children, a dog, a house, children's activities and a social life? No way. Not me. Not going to happen.

Yet, it did.

Somehow I became the black line running through the middle of this family. I don't know if somewhere in my DNA I was programmed for this, or if maybe by default I became the center line for this family. What was the universe thinking—calm and consistent?!

Sigh.

Not what I imagined my life to be.

However, now that I am here, I am working diligently to do a good job. I was always successful in a job situation, so I figure I could be just as successful as the consistent-always-around-going-through-everything-center-black line.

Would you believe me if I told you it's not that easy? And I say that with a smile.

But here's the kicker: I may not look like it, but sometimes, I get really stressed out.

This past summer is the perfect example. I hate to admit it, but I sort of like knowing what is going to happen. I also like knowing that I will not need to physically be in two places at once. (I tried this and I am not "I Dream of Jeannie"!) This summer really tested my abilities to juggle it all while remaining calm and sane. Between traveling, swim team, day camp and a baseball season that seemed never ending, some mornings I woke up and thought, "When will this end?"! Summer is supposed to be fun and laid back and by nearly July I was exhausted.

I also knew I couldn't throw in the towel (because after all, I was the one washing and folding the towels, too). I found myself as the one constant in the household. Everything came through the giant calendar I had posted in the laundry room. None of us made a move without first looking at that calendar.

Even though I wanted to kick back and just take the kids swimming, I still had to make sure we had clean, dry towels, lunches, healthy dinners and books for people to read as well as making sure everyone eventually went to sleep at night. I also had to make sure people were where they needed to be when they needed to be there. Since I am notoriously late (ask any friends), my kids get really bent out of shape if they are late. (I am working on this flaw.) This was perhaps the biggest challenge, because often people needed to be in many places during a day's time, with an entirely new set of clothing.

As summer progressed, I realized that although this indeed might be my life right now, nothing lasts forever. I needed to embrace my responsibilities, make the best of the situation. If need be, I could be... the Boss. I looked around and observed how others were handling it. We were all knee deep in laundry and carpool. As I compared notes with my girlfriends, I realized I was in good company. We might take some time to relax at the pool but for the most part, we were all still parenting throughout the fun.

And the job perks? I just take a look at my own kids. This may be the hardest job I've ever done, but also the most rewarding. I am going to be the *best* Boss I can possibly be. Even if I don't want to be.

Pass me that black crayon.

Curly Girl

One late December morning, I sat in Dan-the-Hair-Man's chair to have my color and highlights fixed. When Dan-the-Hair-Man started to talk about taking my hair back to its original color (which I thought I was actually doing on my own) I became intrigued. After all, Dan-the-Hair-Man was an expert. Who was I to question his expertise and know-how?

My history with my hair is a long, tangled and involved tale. I wish I could say I have always loved my wavy, curly, out-of-control hair. But alas, this is not the case.

For as long as I can remember, I have wanted hair like Marcia Brady's: blonde and oh-so-silky. Remember watching her brushing her hair over and over? Though I tried, my hair never, ever came close. As I got older, my hair got coarser, curlier and wavier.

I was in high school during the era of Christie Brinkley, all blonde and blue-eyed. My wavy, coarse brown hair would never, ever cooperate and never, ever look like hers. I tried everything: sleeping in curlers, hot rollers, coffee cans, and blow drying. No matter what I did, my hair was wavy, long and curly.

In college, I would haul around pictures of Meg Ryan from "When Harry Met Sally." At the end of the movie her hair is all curly and wild. Hair people would say to me again and again, "You don't have that kind of hair." I didn't care. Meg's hair *looked* wavy and curly (was it a perm?) and it was the only hair that looked vaguely close to mine.

I began to wonder what kind of hair I did have. I have been through so many hair people it's a wonder I am allowed back into any salon.

I've been through short (only once and only by mistake, and then I let it grow out for 6 months and it was the cutest it's ever been!), wavy, straight, blonde and blonder (naturally and with a little help), long and then longer, layers, perms and *bad* perms and many, oh-too-many years of ponytails.

Luckily, as I got older, Nicole Kidman and her red curls came along, and soon after that, Sarah Jessica Parker on "Sex and the City" made wavy, wild, curly, somewhat uncontrollable hair acceptable, and (finally!) sought after.

Those women made it okay to *not* have poker-straight blonde hair. Yes, culturally, many other factors made it okay to be exactly who I was with my wild hair, but I like to think it was these self-assured, confident women who said, "I am so much more than my hair."

It took many years to find someone who understood wavy, curly hair and who could cut it really well. That was Maria, and Maria and I were together for about 3 years. Her cuts allowed my hair to curl and be free and happy. I was happy with Maria and she never made any mistakes.

I think it was boredom and curiosity that led me to Dan-the-Hair-Man. My friend Hilary, new to St. Louis, couldn't get an appointment with Maria. She had seen a woman whose hair she liked. So, doing what women do, Hilary asked this woman where she got her hair cut.

Hilary and I have very different hair, but once again, that didn't stop me from having fantasies of something new and different. Change your hair…change your life. (Does everyone think that or is it just me?)

I decided to try Dan-the-Hair-Man. I figured a new set of eyes, someone trained differently, might have an idea about my hair that I hadn't come across yet. I went straight from the gym, all sweaty and wearing a ponytail (even though Hilary told me Dan did *not* approve of ponytails except in the gym), and no make-up. You know, the usual way to get your hair cut.

Surprise. Gasp.

Dan-the-Hair-Man was cute. I mean, really cute. With biceps. And an intense way of listening and giving ideas. Because he did have different ideas. And I was too much in shock not to agree. Well, not entirely true. I bought right into the fantasy again. Everyone in the place, whether cutting and styling or getting cut and styled, was beautiful. They were friendly with everyone, even hugging their customers good-bye. I was, to say the least, a little overwhelmed.

Dan-the-Hair-Man did cut my hair especially well that first time, adding a little more texture to the front, which made a huge difference. When I pulled it back, it was softer, and some of the front hair fell softly over my forehead. I liked the look.

I called Hillary from my car on the way home.

"You didn't tell me he was so hot!" were the first words out of my mouth.

"Who?" Hilary asked.

"Are you kidding me? Dan-the-Hair-Man! He is so hot! And I don't even have make-up on!" She laughed.

Now I am a pretty low-maintenance girl. I often forget to get my hair cut. It was almost 4 months before I returned to Dan-the-Hair-Man, who admonished me, "Please try to remember to come back more than twice a year. Honestly, your hair will look better," he promised with a smile. I knew he was right. Besides, those biceps were fun to watch.

Alas, I am a fluff-and-go girl, so with a good cut, my hair sort of works well for many months. Often I do forget to have it cut.

Though I take risks in other areas of my life, my hair isn't usually one of those places. I have had too many bad cuts and bad perms to go wild anymore. So when Dan-the-Hair-Man started talking about color, it took almost a year for me to consider it.

It was a mistake. When my friends saw me after the Goth-like color was put on (I really thought my natural color was a deep, golden brown, *not* dark brown), they gasped and said, "You changed your hair." See, they should have said that when I cut my hair into a blonde spiky crew cut. *Not when I simply went back to my natural color.*

Dan-the-Hair-Man did eventually fix my hair color. And I did end up liking it quite a bit. It was such a rich, deep brown, and it looked incredibly healthy. However, Dan-the-Hair-Man didn't last, either. It was just too much effort to have to worry about what I looked like to get my hair cut.

Instead I found another kindred soul who understood "curly girls" and have stuck with Valerie ever since. She doesn't try anything too radical; she listens and suggests small steps that I am comfortable with. I think what I love most about Valerie's cuts and colors are that nobody ever sees a difference; my hair always looks natural, healthy and well taken care of. Valerie also has a curly girl soul and I look forward to visiting with her each month. We share a love of our curls, kids and home-made ice cream.

Over time, I have come to terms with my wild, wavy, crazy, uncontrollable hair, even liking and embracing my curly-girl status. I've decided though, women are crazy about their hair, because it is the one thing we think we can control. But as any curly girl knows... curls and waves are not controllable, just manageable. As soon as I embraced that thought...my curly-girl really started living.

Hi-Ho, Silver!

It was my daughter Jessie's idea.

I'm not sure how she came up with it, but when I asked, "Is there anything we haven't done in Scouts?" she replied, "I'd like to try horseback riding."

Great request.

Horrible idea.

I had a bad experience on a horse more than twenty years ago, and the only horses I've been near since are those at the Faust Park Carousel.

So I stalled. Then in April I planned for the Scouts to stay over at Père Marquette Park to celebrate the end of five successful, fun years together. On the park website was a link to the Stables.

Like the good cowgirl I so wanted to be, I called.

Magically, Père Marquette Stables, two miles from the park and lodge, offered horseback riding. When I contacted them, they said they would love to have us in May. As I talked further with Kit (the owner and resident cowboy) I began to slowly trust him. He answered all my questions thoroughly, had ideas of his own, and generally seemed like a trustworthy cowboy. About the third or fourth time I spoke with him, I mentioned that I would need a gentle old "glue" horse that was slow and kind.

He laughed. "Remind me when you get here," was all he would promise.

Because we had so many girls going, we had to split into two groups. They had enough horses, just not enough saddles for so many kids.

Gail, the other adult going on the trip with us, volunteered to go twice if I wasn't going to ride.

I decided to leave that decision to the moment.

So here's my thing. I honestly admire horses and those people who ride. I think that horses are beautiful animals and I would like nothing better than to be a cowgirl (and dress like one). However, I haven't ridden since that bad experience. And really, when would I have the opportunity? If you aren't a horse person, you don't seek horse-type adventures.

I'm not sure what I'm frightened of. Could it be that the horse is just so big? That the horse has a mind of his own? That I could get thrown? Or am I just a wuss? All good thoughts…I decided to go with my gut once we got there.

We got to the stables and the first group saddled up. As they left and I watched my 11-year-old daughter ride away on her horse, happy and confident, I still hadn't made up my mind what I might do.

The first group came back and the second group put their helmets on and saddled up. When it was my turn, Kit very matter of factly helped me up onto Duke. Hmmm, didn't feel so bad. Didn't feel so scary. Duke was big, but Kit assured me he was gentle. I thought maybe I actually could do this. What was so bad about this anyway?…I'll tell you.

They freed Duke, and as he started walking I thought my stomach was going to leave through my ears. Duke walked. I wobbled side to side. Being a trail horse, good ol' Duke knew exactly what to do and followed the horse in front of him. I tried to breathe calmly and not panic. The more I thought about panicking, the more I realized I was going to. I concentrated hard on the instructions Kit had given me.

After about fifteen minutes, Kit asked me if I was beginning to relax a little. Well, yes, as a matter of fact, I was relaxing. Just a little. I didn't mind wobbling and I didn't mind being up so *high*. Duke knew what to do and was doing it. He readily followed my instructions. What do you think about that?!

And then Duke galloped to catch up and I thought it was going to be the end of me. Galloping! I held on (with my legs and hands) and then, just as suddenly as he'd started, Duke settled back into a gentle walk.

I was okay. I was still *on* Duke.

Kit and the other cowboys taught us how to guide the horses, pick up the pace and stop them. I know this is crazy, but after a while, it wasn't so scary for me to ask Duke to gallop. In fact, I sort of liked it. Maybe I actually *am* a cowgirl.

I suddenly "got" the fascination with horses. You definitely got from point A to point B faster than walking. But it wasn't only practical. I understood how amazing it was to be on a horse and not be scared. I don't think I lost my fear completely, but I did let it go long enough to enjoy the almost hour-long trail ride.

In fact, I enjoyed the ride so much I could see myself going back to Père Marquette Stables and riding more. The trails were beautiful and tranquil and I loved talking with the cowboys.

More than anything, I was very proud that at this late stage of the game, I had attempted to do something that for so long had brought fear to my heart. I could have easily decided not to ride. But then I wouldn't have felt the exhilaration of getting out of my saddle and thanking Duke for a good ride.

I wouldn't have conquered this part of my story.

Just call me Annie Oakley…suburban cowgirl.

Own It!

On a recent all-girls weekend at the lake, as we were preparing breakfast, I nibbled the white chocolate cheesecake someone had brought. It was a perfect wake-me-up.

"Oh Pam," my friend Anne laughed. "You really do have issues with delayed gratification!"

"What does that mean?" I asked, although I already knew.

"Dessert before breakfast."

"You know... I've decided to own it! I'm 48 years old. I love dessert. If I don't own this now, eating dessert first (or last or in between), when will I?" I asked.

From that moment on I began to assess what else I could now proudly *own* and something in me was freed. I do eat a lot of desserts. On the other hand, why not? I wasn't infringing on anyone else's rights and I do try to exercise every day, so why not eat dessert first? Why not own up to everything that makes me happy?

In the spirit of living free, I thought that this year, I would own all the quirky characteristics that make me *me*.

Eating dessert first. Okay, first, *you are what you eat*. If this is true, I am a huge chocolate chip cookie, a mint ice cream sundae, or a New York cheesecake. I don't care which one: it's a win-win situation.

Eating only dessert. Who does this really bother? And if it makes me happy sometimes, the world will go on. Besides, woman can live on salad alone for only so long.

Being crabby. Yes, sometimes I am. However, if you give me enough time or I can take a walk, I can work myself out of it. Everyone is entitled to a crabby moment...or two.

I don't do mornings. Honestly, I can't think in the middle of the night and until I've been up for a little while, mornings aren't my thing. Having said that, I love sunrises.

Yes, I am a Brady enthusiast. I love the Brady Bunch. I've seen every incarnation and my sister and I can recite lines from any episode. It doesn't matter how old I get, I will always love the Bradys...and David Cassidy.

Reading is my escape. I don't like organized book groups because often I can't keep up with someone else's schedule and I probably won't like all the books the group chooses to read. I love to talk about books, but in a casual way. I love to read, but I am choosy. I read books about strong women who triumph in the end. I tend to read books by women authors. I don't buy books to sit on the shelf. I like books that capture my attention right away. If I read thirty pages and can't get into it, I return the book to the library. I don't feel the need to keep up with what everyone else is reading. Reading is *mine and honestly...one of my survival strategies!*

Enough with the school lunches. In my lifetime as a parent, I believe I have made four million peanut butter and jelly sandwiches. Please. Buy lunch every now and then. Or, better yet, *make your own.*

No more Drama Mamas. Seriously. If you are going to bring drama into my world–don't. I am not interested. Quit trying to live through your daughters and get a life already. And, please, keep your drama to yourself.

Working out. I love to work out. Well, I love what exercising does for my psyche and my thighs. Leave me alone already. I work out when I can. And besides, I don't pass judgment on you and what you love to do.

Dancing with my friends. Sometimes you just have to let loose and shake your groove thing to 80s music.

80s Music. I Love it. Love it. Love it. I don't care that you can tell when I went to high school. I love Duran Duran, Madonna, The Go-Gos. It's the music I grew up with and I want to dance all night to it. If I want to sing at the top of my lungs while driving down Highway 40, I'll do that, too.

Game playing. Count me in for Scrabble or gin rummy. Just count me *out* for whatever catty-exclusionary-witchy game you're playing. I mean what I say and say what I mean and I'm not playing your games. I've already been to high school. So find someone else to play with you. It's not fun and I'm *out*.

Wearing last year's "gotta-have-it-item". Hello! I'm a suburban mom (even though I fantasize about being a city girl). I *like* my boyfriend jeans. Finally a pair of jeans that aren't made for skinny girls without hips. My boyfriend jeans look good on me. They allow me to sit down, stand up, and–most important–breathe.

Hello, world! Here I am, in my boyfriend jeans, eating dessert first with my dancing girlfriends. It's a rockin' good life!

My Secret Life as a Pole Dancer

It's no secret that I love to dance. Most any kind of dancing is fine by me. I love music and the sheer joy of movement. I will try any kind of dance and in the last few years I have attempted modern, hip-hop, tap, ballet, salsa, belly dancing and Zumba.

Because I can, I imagine myself to be Jennifer Beals in "Flashdance," disguised as a softball mom. Or Jennifer Gray in "Dirty Dancing," undercover as a room parent. I managed to perpetuate my fantasy when I tried a jazz class at a community college. I love jazz. It is as close to Broadway as I will ever get. I like to think that in another life I could have been a Broadway dancer. I can do the basic moves, but what I enjoyed most were the leaps, jumps and turns. I flew through the air and loved it. For some reason, I could master the steps without injuring myself.

Last summer I enjoyed a Salsa Funk class at my gym. I really had no idea what to expect. I sneaked a few peeks and decided to try it. Kim, the instructor, oozes fun while shaking her groove thing. She easily got us going with salsa. Soon we were all shaking and whoo-hooing and using our booties to burn calories and have a good time. I love exercising to music because it doesn't feel like exercise. Kim kept us moving, grooving and dancing the entire hour.

At the end of class, Kim treated us to hip-hop. I have to be honest. I have never done hip-hop, although I am fascinated by it. As time went on, I learned to like the attitude of the dance as much as the choreography. Kim has now switched over to Zumba and I am a loyal devotee. An hour of dancing twice a week, burning calories and having fun is a great way to exercise. I knew I loved disco, but had no idea that country, Cha-Cha and Merengue could be *so* much fun, too. Swiveling across the floor as if we are in a music video brings me such happiness.

Last March, my sister and I took a Pole Dancing class. Yes, you read that right. While looking for a fund-raising idea, I stumbled upon The Fitness Studio, which offers cardio fitness, boot camp, and pole dancing classes. I immediately signed up for their e-mails, and every month I got a flyer about pole dancing workshops. One Saturday in March we had no plans. I promptly called my sister, who is my sidekick in most of my adventures these days.

"Want to try a pole dancing class?" I asked. I already knew the answer.

"Sure!" she replied. I smiled.

I signed us up, picked her up on Saturday and off we went to our first pole dancing class. When we got there, we saw that there were two poles in the gym. After a warm-up dance, Shannon, our instructor showed us our first pole move.

Okay, stop here.

Our "first pole move." I felt like I was in an alternate world.

And it felt good!

Shannon danced around the pole and hopped up onto it, spinning around.

"Okay, who's first?" she asked.

I stepped up to the pole, trying to figure out exactly how I was supposed to lift myself on to it. Shannon patiently explained again (this would become a theme) and I tried it. Hmmm, not bad for a beginner. At this point I decided to put on my heels. The studio asks you to bring heels and honestly? It is so much easier to pole dance in heels.

Stop again.

"So much easier to pole dance in heels." Now there's a line I never thought I would think, much less write.

We learned about five moves. Some were progressions of previous moves, some completely new. I found some of the pole moves incredibly challenging. For example, I have very little flexibility in my back, so curving over my back while holding myself on the pole was hard for me. However, I was able to do the "cradle" easily. You start by hopping up onto the pole and spinning around. (You don't have to visualize that.) I was also able to do this spinning move with my leg out by holding myself on the pole with my abs. It was fun to start by walking around the pole and then flipping up onto the pole. Yes! I could do that one, too!

At about this time, I was dripping with sweat, my sister was busy doing her pole moves and I realized that we were having a great time. The class was comprised of eight women, all of us at different fitness levels, heights, weights and experience. Though we didn't know one another, we cheered each other on as one by one we practiced our moves on the poles.

I love trying something outside my comfort zone. (I probably won't ever sky dive, but I will try most any kind of dance class.) I really enjoy dancing and the different way my body moves. Over time, I have learned that when dancing, attitude and the willingness to just *let go* is even more important than mastering any dance technique.

In fact, I can now say that I am becoming a more confident dancer. Seriously, if you don't gain some sort of confidence after dancing on a pole, I'm not sure what will do it for you. By the way, we did tell our kids what we had done, and there is nothing funnier than seeing your teenage son's face when you tell him that his mom learned pole dancing.

Lately, when I've been out dancing with girlfriends, I realize that salsa, Zumba and hip-hop lend themselves to feeling free and I move my body in a completely different way.

What a feeling! I hear music now…

What I Did for Love

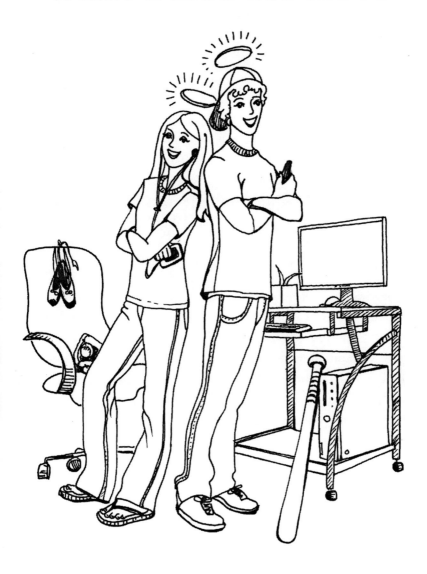

Life Lessons From the Princess Game

Much to my surprise, my first child was a boy. I was raised with girls. We had no experience with boys. Having a son has been a learning experience, especially the rough-and-tumble physical play.

My second child was a girl. "Aha," I thought. "Now I know exactly what to do."

I was determined to raise both kids without any preconceived notions of what little boys and little girls were supposed to be like. We had the same toys and games which both kids loved. They wore the same clothing, handed down from Joe to Jessie. I could always throw a pink bow in her hair, or add a headband, but I never needed to. I just figured clothes were clothes. Jessie knew who she was even if she was wearing her brother's old jeans.

Because my daughter was the second child and very easygoing, my son used her as a prop in his play. She learned everything she needed to know from him. He had a great imagination and always included anyone around him, including his sister. They played restaurant, cooking and superhero. Since a lot of the neighborhood kids were boys, Jessie learned to play whatever they were into, and it usually involved plenty of physical action. She climbed and ran early and often, and she could really swing a baseball bat.

Then she went to preschool, in a class with amazing teachers and an even lovelier group of children. My daughter thrived in this group. She loved school and everything that they did. She was introduced to many different activities and kinds of play. For the most part, she gets right into whatever is going on. But, much to my chagrin, she was also introduced to princess play.

You read that right: princess play. (Sigh.) How could a daughter of mine be interested in princesses? In college, I studied early childhood education. I knew all the right ways to stimulate androgynous thinking, and all the right activities to promote children's growth and learning. I would rather see "Independent Thinking Woman" blaze across her chest than any princess message.

Well, whether I liked it or not, play in the 4-year-old classroom was all about princesses. I was completely surprised when one day my daughter innocently asked me whether I knew that Ariel was a princess *and* a mermaid. There it was. She carefully watched for my reaction.

This is the little girl who loves to wear her brother's old clothes, who hates dresses and hates to wear bows in her waist-length blonde hair. She loves to follow her brother up mountainsides, into the deep end of the swimming pool and around the block on her bicycle. This little girl is not a girly-girl. She can't wait to play baseball on a team, can run with the best of them and holds her own when a bigger child gets in her space.

Where did I go wrong?

I could hardly wait to talk with my friend Jenny, who has three daughters. I was so relieved to learn that her two older girls were into princesses in preschool, but today they play soccer and would much rather see Mia Hamm than "Princesses on Ice."

When my son was the same age, I knew every type of dinosaur. I knew their special characteristics, what families they lived in and what they ate. I was on a first-name basis with both the brachiosaurus and the triceratops. I guess I could learn about princesses. I just didn't want to shut down the play or her interests. How bad could it be?

I tried to keep an open mind about learning the princess stories. I have to admit: I didn't love it. When my daughter received the Princess Game at her fourth birthday party, I thought, "Oh! Now I can really learn about these chicks." And I did. I learned their gowns and jewelry, their powers (they all possess certain powers, and most are *not* supernatural!) and each corresponding Prince Charming.

I decided to focus on each princess's positive quality. Ariel the mermaid was incredibly caring and Snow White very kindhearted. Cinderella believed in her ability to make her dreams come true, and (my favorite) Belle was super intelligent–both book smart and people smart. These were the characteristics I played up whenever talk turned to princesses. I was hoping my daughter would interject some of this century's sensibilities and my own bias into her play.

Deep into winter, I discovered that princess play did not occupy all my daughter's time. She played games, did puzzles, flew kites and still followed her brother up mountainsides and around the block.

With each goodnight kiss, I remind my daughter that she is an independent woman making her own choices and doing whatever she wants in the world. She is free and strong, kind and funny. And while my words serve a purpose, I am reminded that the princess game, too, served a purpose for her.

Perhaps we free-thinking women (as well as our daughters) can learn some important life lessons from pretending to be a princess.

First, we can make our dreams come true without Prince Charming's assistance. Snow White probably would have woken up when she got hungry enough.

Second, if you don't get what you want the first time you roll the dice, roll again. Decide what you want and go after it. Ariel the mermaid wanted to be human. She risked just about everything to give it a try. She learned that she needed to risk just enough of herself to find what she really wanted.

Third, going to the ball is nice, but getting yourself there is just as important.

Finally, if we really believe in ourselves, Tinkerbell's magic fairy dust can propel us to heights we've only just begun to dream of. We don't really need a magic wand; we just need our dreams and the confidence to take risks. I learned through all the princess play that if those dreams for a 4-year-old come in the form of a princess, so be it. In time princesses would give way to Harry Potter, vampires and pitching softball.

You Throw Like a Girl

Springtime two years ago, my son Joe joined a baseball team for the first time and he loved it. He wanted to throw and catch all the time. That Mother's Day, I received perfume, chocolate (because all celebrations mandate chocolate for me) and a catcher's glove.

I took one look at it and knew this was going to be quite a challenge. I did not play sports growing up. When I was in high school, the only sports being played by girls were tennis or field hockey. I figured I had mastered nursing, diapering, playgroups and preschool. With some help, I could figure this out.

Help came in the form of a six-year-old named Joe. One of the best guys around. He worked with me day after day, throwing me fastballs, slow balls, curve balls and the deadly fly balls. He gave me pointers in how to move my wrist and my arm to better use my glove. He yelled at me to move right or left or backward or forward.

One day, when he wanted to have catching practice, he said I should throw the ball to him. I happily obliged.

"Mom," he said quite innocently, "you throw like a girl!"

"I am a girl!" I shouted.

He looked at me and realization spread across his face. I was, in fact, a girl.

I had noticed a long time ago that my first-born was a boy. It was a surprise to me all those years ago and it still is today; I am often surprised to find myself among a group of boys.

I knew nothing about little boys. Instinctively though I knew if I mothered him to the best of my ability, I would raise a well-adjusted, happy person, regardless of sex.

When Joe was 7 ½ I realized that I had a wealth of knowledge about boys...

Boys smell different than girls. That's not to say that all kids don't smell sweaty, but boys in particular have a distinctive odor. Sometime around 4, they lose that toddler smell. I know this, because my friend Karen still has a toddler and he still smells like soap. Sometimes all it takes is a shower and Joe is good to go.

Boys use their laundry basket as another storage unit. It doesn't matter if clothes are in the laundry basket completely filthy. If that's the shirt Joe is looking for, that's the shirt he wears. Often, I will say, "Is that from your laundry basket?" sheepishly he will grin and nod yes.

Little boys love to wrestle. Boys are like puppies, learning socialization through wrestling. Joe will wrestle with anyone at any time. He loves wrestling with his dad, his sister, friends and one very obliging babysitter.

Boys forgive. If you have a son, you know exactly what I mean. Joe once told me, "Why can't girls be more like boys? We slug it out and hug it out." I've seen this happen time and again and being a girl, I am always astonished that they really do forgive and forget.

Boys try anything. Just because. When Joe was about 7 or 8, I looked out the back window and found Joe and a friend walking across the monkey bars. Walking ACROSS bars that were nine feet high. They waved at me. Their sense of adventure is awe-inspiring...even at age 7.

Boys are completely unorganized and have no shame in this. We joke in our house that the uterus is simply a homing device and if you don't have one you can't find anything. Once when Joe was looking for something in the pantry, I heard him mutter, "If I had a uterus, I could find this....but I can balance a check book!" Needless to say, the battle lines are drawn in this area.

I've learned a lot in the seven years a boy now lives here. It's been fun and interesting. Regardless if Joe realizes I'm a girl I am happy to learn to catch and throw. In fact, I look at his teaching me as a gift. That glove was and still is one of my favorite Mother's Day presents ever. It's like earning my mothering stripes...I can catch and throw... like a girl.

Look, Mom! No Hands!

Jessie, my five-year-old daughter, just learned to ride her two-wheeler *sans* training wheels. It wasn't as long a journey as some kids take, and wasn't as easy for her as it is for some kids.

I asked her if she wanted to try about a month ago. She agreed, but then once on the bike got very scared very quickly which is very unlike her. She didn't want to try again. I borrowed a "tag-along" for my bicycle so she could get the feel of balancing while safe in the security of my handling.

Two days ago, she asked if she could try her bicycle without the training wheels. She got on, and with arms encircling her, she rode away on her own. She didn't get very far before putting her feet down to steady herself, but she rode, and she balanced on her own.

Today, she is riding circles with her brother and friends. She has now been riding for almost two hours, sometimes happily, sometimes so frustrated she yells at the bicycle. She is keeping her balance while watching out for other cyclists and having a great time.

Meanwhile her 7-½-year-old brother is shouting to me, "Look Mom! No, hands!" and when I smile and encourage him, he changes tactics, "Look Mom! No hands *and* no feet!" Sure enough, he is now standing on his bicycle seat, steering and trying to keep his balance. He, too, is figuring out how to balance while taking risks and having a great time.

While I am outside, Jessie asks for help to get started. Joe whizzes by me so fast that I can't even capture him on film. Their friends are going every which way, and everyone is having as much fun as you can when you are five or seven, riding your bicycle with friends after school on a beautiful spring afternoon in St. Louis.

As I watch Jessie start and stop and start again, it occurs to me that learning to ride a bicycle is a lot like parenting.

It's hands-on and hands-off so quickly that it makes your head spin.

It's being immensely proud of your child's determination and sheer will while taking a step back because it has absolutely nothing to do with you. I cannot take credit for either of my children being able to ride their bikes. I can take credit for offering support, encouraging them to push themselves to try new activities, for bandaging scraped knees and kissing bruised egos.

It's a fine line to walk between my own ideas and letting my kids be who they are and become who they can be.

I am not very good at this. I know all the appropriate child development techniques. I am very good at this with other kids. It's just that, with my own children, well, it's different. Often, I find that the best moments in our lives as parents are those times when we just let our kids… BE.

For me, particularly, when I let them find their own balance, those are the times I know that I am doing everything completely…okay.

Sometimes I have to swallow my words back. I don't ever want to program my kids into thinking that they can or cannot do something. I want them to try it all: climbing the tallest tree, spelling the hardest word, running a mile, reading a book that's one level too hard. How else will they ever learn what they can accomplish? How else will they conquer everything they want to try if I don't continue to encircle them in my love, support them, and then let them go?

Like when my children began their journey on their two-wheelers. I encircled them with my arms and then… I let go. I am always a shout away. And it's usually me shouting, "You go, girl!" or "Way to go, Joe!"

When they are finding out who they are by exploring what it feels like to stand on the seat of a bicycle and yes, possibly falling, you will find me on the sidelines, cheering and smiling and feeling blessed.

I know their limits. I know in my head and my heart what they can do, and I hope they continue to try. Sometimes, the sheer will of my children is daunting. I have felt if first-hand while watching them master their bicycles, write reports about blue whales, and try to persuade me that Pop Tarts are a food group.

I imagine that letting go is the hardest part for most of us. My heart knows all too well that while today it is a bicycle, tomorrow it is a car, and after that it is leaving home. I silently shout my encouragement: "Keep riding, Jess, keep going." And my heart bursts with love for my daughter, who simply will not give up until she is riding on her own.

Locks of Love

It was the day before Thanksgiving. For the second time in fourteen months, I found myself sitting at The Face and The Body to watch as my eight-year old-daughter had ten inches of hair cut off to donate to Locks of Love, the program that makes wigs for children with cancer who have lost their hair as a result of illness.

It wasn't my idea; it was hers. She was seven years old, and one day she announced that she wanted to cut her hair and donate it. Ten inches of her beautiful hair. I was devastated.

Which says so much more about me than I want revealed.

I have thick-curly-wavy-out-of-control hair. I always have. I grew up in the time of Christie Brinkley and the Breck girl. Not one of the Breck girls had curly, wavy, dark hair; theirs was always light and shiny. It has been only within the last few years that curly, wavy hair has been celebrated. Thank you, Sarah Jessica Parker!

So when I had a daughter who turned out to be incredibly blonde, I was amazed. Jessie has Marcia Brady hair: shiny, smooth, lots of body and light blonde. We never cut it. When she was little, there was no need; we just let it grow and grow. By the time she was seven, her hair had been trimmed maybe three times.

As her hair grew out blonde and shiny it was prettier than mine had ever been. I secretly want to take her with me when I have the gray washed out so that I could point to it and say, "Can you do this?" For her part, Jessie just wanted it out of her face. "Just make a ponytail, mom!" was her response to my suggestions for fancy hairstyles.

Once I made the appointment for her haircut, I kept trying to give her an out. "You don't have to do this. We can just get it trimmed,"

I said (oh so casually) more than once. "Mom, I'm doing something good for another child," my seven-year-old daughter always replied, looking me full in the eyes with those crystal clear blues ones.

So in July our family trooped over to The Face and The Body for the big cut. Oh yes, it was a family affair. I had my camera. Joe looked bored. I was shaking. I didn't know if I wanted this beautiful hair to be cut. But, it wasn't my hair, it was hers, and she had made her decision. I trusted Jessie, even at 7 years old, to make good decisions.

Knowing this was a Locks of Love cut, the people at the salon treated Jessie as an extra-special customer. Jamie, the stylist, gathered Jessie's hair into four ponytails and then asked if we were ready. Jessie replied that she was. Jamie snipped as I snapped a photo. I wanted to cry, but didn't.

Jamie looked at me. "You okay, mom?" She asked. I smiled bravely. (How many times am I going to be required to smile bravely as a parent?)

Jamie proceeded to cut the other three ponytails. Jessie's hair came to just below her shoulders. Then Jamie asked Jessie if she wanted to hold her cut-off ponytails. Nope. Jamie washed her hair and then evened up the cut.

It was a really cute cut. And after a few days of struggle, we figured out how to fashion it into a ponytail. Life went on.

When I look at the pictures from that day, I realize how cute her haircut was and I am also floored by the amazing thing she did at age seven.

Here's the thing. Jessie is not attached to her hair as I am. Apparently– and I'm not telling you anything new here–some women feel that their hair gives them their identity. It makes them who they are. I am one of them. I like to have good hair days. They put an extra bounce in my walk.

Fast forward fourteen months. "Mom, it's time to cut my hair for Locks of Love again," Jessie told me. I measured, and sure enough we were almost at the required ten inches. Not quite. "We need to let it grow a few more inches or it will be too short," I said.

By November 2009, we were there. She had ten inches of hair to spare. This time, however, when they put the ponytails in, I gasped out loud without even realizing I'd done it. Lauren, the stylist turned to look at me. "This is ten inches," she said holding up a ruler. "Oh, I believe you," I replied. "I just thought it was longer." She moved the ponytails down a little. She looked at Jessie. "What do you think?"

Jessie didn't blink an eye. "It's okay," she said looking at both me and the stylist. Lauren glanced back at me. "Jessie, if you want to wait a month we can," I said to her.

"No, Mom, its okay."

Lauren cut, and seriously, I thought I was going to pass out. So much for my tolerance level for stress. It was short. Really short.

"I'm going to give her a little bob," Lauren reassured me.

As the final ponytail was cut, Jessie began to swing her hair back and forth…like a Breck girl. Like Marcia Brady.

True to her word, after Lauren washed Jessie's hair, she cut a bob and then dried it. It could not have been cuter (and neither could she!) and off we went for Thanksgiving weekend.

About ten o'clock that evening we heard a little mouse coming downstairs. The cries, however, were not so little.

"My hair is too short! Everyone is going to laugh at me!" She was inconsolable. Kenny and I hugged her and tripped over our words as we tried to reassure her. "You did something so nice and generous for another child!" said Kenny. "Your hair is really cute and it will grow," I soothed.

By the time she went to school on Monday, with her hair pushed back with a cute headband (no ponytails for awhile), Jessie was herself again; ready to take on the world. Our bright and shining incredibly generous Breck girl.

Lift-Off

When my son Joe was 12-½ and coming home from sleep-away camp he informed me that all the friends from his cabin would soon be sending him Bar Mitzvah invitations. I nodded. As the fall progressed, no invites showed up and I was just as happy to keep it that way.

One day as he hopped into my car, I overheard Joe saying on the phone, "I'll have to check with my parents." Hmm. I hadn't heard him say *that* in a long time. It was usually, "Can I do this/that?" and I had to makeadecisionrightthen!

"That was my friend Braden and he and I have worked out how I can stay at his house when I go to Minneapolis. His parents said it was fine." I wanted to tell Joe to breathe, but he kept going, "I should be getting an invitation any day."

Again, I just nodded and said nothing.

A few days later, sure enough, an invitation from Minneapolis arrived for Joe. He was beside himself with excitement. This was really happening. He actually got an invitation. "Can I go?" he asked, hopping on one leg.

"I don't know," I answered.

"We have it all worked out. I can stay with my friend. You just have to call his parents."

That's it, huh? Just call the parents of a friend that I have never met or talked to. Somehow *get* Joe to Minneapolis. Figure out how to make it all work, long distance and oh yes, *let go*.

We tabled it for some weeks. I just couldn't fathom putting my child, the child I knew from the time he was a speck, the child I grew in my womb, on a plane alone. And then saying goodbye! I wouldn't even be able to go to the airport to see him off. I would never, ever be able to do this.

It reminded me of the first day of preschool. "Mommies always come back," was my mantra. This time, though, I kept thinking, "baby birds always come back, right?" They do, don't they?

Finally, we were down to the wire and I called the parents of Joe's friend. Honestly, they couldn't have been nicer or more accommodating and as it happened they were quite comfortable with the boys' plan. They invited Joe to stay for the entire weekend.

It took me some time to think all this through and be okay. I had flown by myself at age 8, but that was in a different world. So many things would be out of my control. So many fears about my child's safety that if I began to think about it, I wouldn't be able to sleep.

My kids have always been one step ahead of me at every age and every stage. *They* are the ones dragging *me* along while I wonder how we got to where we are. What happened to my baby birds? When did they grow old enough to travel on their own?

Joe had absolutely no fear about hopping on a plane and spending the weekend with a friend in another state. None. In fact, he was barely able to contain his excitement and started a countdown. Each day, I would hear how many days until lift-off.

As it turned out, Joe was fine. In fact, he hadthebestweekendever. The family he stayed with kept in close touch with us, so Joe was "alone" only for the two hours he flew each way.

And Mama Bird? Well, I didn't go to the airport to drop him off, but I did keep my phone close. I didn't exhale the whole two hours he flew on Friday. I wasn't truly at ease until he walked off that plane and into my waiting arms on Sunday night.

Mission accomplished. (Until next time.)

Son of Man

Dear Joe,

On your thirteenth birthday, I wanted to let you know how I feel about having a teenager, an almost-man, living in the house. I clearly remember what it was like thirteen years ago, craving French toast and steak and wondering who you would be and what you would be like.

On a hot June 11th, nine days after the doctor had estimated you would arrive, I awoke to contractions. It would be 32 more hours before you arrived, and that was only after much visualization, repeated affirmations that I wanted you to be born without surgical intervention and incredible excitement.

I took one look at you, and my life changed. Completely. Incredibly. Wholeheartedly. Forever. I had waited all my life for you. I knew in my heart that we were meant to be together. I didn't know why, but I was confident that, in time, I would find out.

We went home, and after three days we were left alone to fend for ourselves. I actually think that you and I slept through that first summer. In September, we started to get out of the house more. Wherever we went, we made friends, as you engaged everyone you met with your happy smile. From the beginning, you had these huge, blue eyes, and by the time you were five months' old, dark, curly masses of hair. You talked to everybody and they all smiled back. Is that how you first figured out the world?

You loved being outside at the park and the swimming pool, and had no fear about trying new things. You adored Starr, our first dog, and in fact, your first word was "Starr." (That's okay, Joe, I didn't really mind the 32-hour labor.)

When you were in kindergarten, I wondered if you would ever learn to read, and now you read voraciously. In third grade, we endlessly went over your multiplication tables, and I wondered if you would ever know those. And here we are today, in challenge math. When you went to camp for the first time, I couldn't believe you were all of ten years old, going into fifth grade, but you came back after two weeks and said, "That was the best time of my life. I'm going back all summer!"

The years have flown by.

I look at you today, my almost-man, and I am in awe at the person you have become. More and more, you remind me of Grandpa Phil and the entire line of Wilson men. You have all the characteristics: independence, intelligence, curiosity, and a sense of humor. Like them, you are fun to be around. And like them, you always have an agenda. I often laugh that my reason for being is to facilitate your agendas.

Having an almost-man is like having a big three-year-old in the house. You would not believe how many of the behaviors are similar. (And so are my reactions!) I have watched you learn to make good decisions for yourself despite what others may choose to do. I have happily witnessed you standing up for what you believe in.

As you continue on this journey from boy to man, remember that it is the people you meet and the adventures you have that make your journey worthwhile. Always treat everyone (especially girls) with the utmost care. Treat them how you want to be treated–it will always come back to you. Always answer a phone call. Try to be the best friend to others that you can be. Think globally, act locally. Be true to yourself, no matter what.

One of my favorite characters is the Disney Tarzan, who learns to be a man with the help of an entire community. We have tried to do that for you, too, with our family and friends. You remind me of Tarzan as he grows into a man in the song, "Son of Man" especially as you grow into the man I always knew you would become. I love the part when Phil Collins sings:

"In learning you will teach and in teaching you will learn. Lift your spirits and be free, a man in time you'll be. Son of man, a man for all to see."

I love you, Joe—now, forever and always. Happy thirteenth birthday!

Love, Mom.

Sweet Child O' Mine

"Stop treating me like a baby," Jessie said, as she stomped out of the bathroom at the Muny this summer. "I'm not treating you like a baby," I answered. "This is a very public place and you can't wander around without me." The discussion was in response to my not letting my 11-½-year-old daughter wait for me *outside* the bathroom.

At the deepest level of motherhood, I knew she was right. My head knew it, but my heart, funny thing that it is, didn't want to know it.

During intermission, when we again paid a visit to the bathroom, I casually said, "Just wait for me right out here," which she happily did. We've been doing it this way ever since.

There have been other changes. Small, casual changes that she has pushed on me this summer. She now wants to do her own hair. For almost eleven years, she would hand me a brush and ask for a ponytail or braids. The end of this school year found me having to stand on a stair to be tall enough to gather her tresses into a ponytail. This summer, I've done fewer ponytails than ever before.

Jessie now has her own ideas about what she wants to wear. For years, she would request that I just pull something out of the closet for her. This was actually quite easy, because all she wore were hand-me-down T-shirts from her brother and soccer shorts to her knees. Suddenly, she's fascinated with other kinds of clothes. She's just wandering into this area. Everything can be mixed and matched (I tried to make this part easy), and she wants to handle it on her own. Quite honestly, she has her own unique style.

From the beginning, my husband, Kenny, and I wanted to ensure that our kids would be able to make choices for themselves. We help the kids look at all their options and then make a decision everyone can live with. "Do you want peanut butter and jelly or grilled cheese?" has become, "Would you like to go the pool today or invite a friend over?" I realized somewhat quickly that Jessie is quite an independent person. She has pretty much always marched to her own drummer and only asks for input when she wants it. I adore independent children, but I also miss having little kids around.

Because I don't have little kids anymore. I have a full-fledged teenager (!) and a preteen. And they are both giving me a run for my money.

In my case, I simply have to keep up. Jessie is now reading books for preteens and understanding all the underlying themes, but still she *loved* the movie "Ramona and Beezus." Jessie now wonders why some of her friends are becoming more interested in boys as more than friends; she still wants to swim and play kickball with everyone. She is a textbook case of the preteen.

The way I see it, I have two choices.

I could deny Jessie this rite of passage. Simply ignore the fact that she is indeed growing up and needs a mom who knows the score. I could just keep my head in the sand and pretend that she is still a little girl.

Or I can embrace this change in her life and grow with her. I can be a mom who will listen, ask questions and provide boundaries and rules that are fair and equitable to this age and stage. But I can still make ice cream and play gin rummy with her.

I knew my days were numbered earlier this spring when, as we walked into a park filled with her peers, I tried to hold her hand. She pulled away from me with a look that said, "Are you kidding me?!" And yet, later that *same* day when we ran to the mall on a quick errand, she allowed me to take her hand and even swing it. I haven't tried again, although sometimes she will spontaneously lean against me when we are watching movies. Fortunately, she still allows herself to be kissed goodnight.

I choose Door #2! I choose to grow and revel in each and every stage of her growth and development. I can do this; I know I can. I can parent a preteen as well as I parented a little girl. Frankly, I could really use a "What to Expect from Your Pre-teen" volume about now.

She may no longer be a baby (or a toddler or a preschooler); however, this version of my sweet child of mine will forever live in my heart. The real Jessie, on the other hand, will grow and change and continue to become an amazing young woman whom I catch glimpses of every now and then. And lucky me, I'll be right here beside her.

The Game of Life

On a beautiful Friday in August, I was lucky enough to be at the community swimming pool with a book, my daughter and two of her lifelong friends. We staked claim to some pool chairs and the kids were off. It was a good thing that I had an interesting book to read, because I didn't see them again until they were hungry for lunch, then snack. At about five o'clock, they were ready to go home.

We were having a "More the Merrier" day together. About a month earlier we were all at the pool together and when we got back to my house, they pulled out board games, including Life. If you have never witnessed eleven-year-olds playing "The Game of Life," please, make sure that at some point you do. It was hysterical to listen to them making choices and deciding what to do about Life. At one point someone stated, "Are we even playing this right?" while another girl asked for the directions.

Unfortunately, none of us planned on this sort of marathon day, and the girls reluctantly cleaned up the game. "Would you all like to have another day like this?" I asked. "We can start at the pool, stay as long as you like, and then come back here for games and dinner."

You would have thought I had offered them a trip to Disney World. All three happily said yes, and their moms and I went about finding a day that would work for all three of them. We found one Friday in August and penciled it onto the calendar.

I was happy to have the girls all day and into the evening. Tamar, Rachel, and my daughter, Jessie, have been friends since they were tots. Rachel's mom, Diane, and I were friendly, having girls at the same time. Rachel and Jessie met Tamar in preschool, and over the years, they have stayed close. Once I met Karen, Tamar's mom, I knew I had also found a friend for life.

Two interesting things strike me. First, a cross word is never spoken when the girls are together. They are loving, fun, creative, and mischievous, but never have they fought. I know that sounds strange, but they get along really well. The other interesting aspect of their relationship is that their boundaries are permeable and flexible. They welcome other girls into and out of their circle–at home, at camp, at the pool. They always have room for one more and never hesitate to include anyone else. For some reason, the threesome works with this group of girls. They aren't "BFFs" by any stretch of the imagination. This friendship is almost on a different level, and while I am with them, I am just astonished that at this young age, they are happy simply to be with one another, enjoying the day, the games, the sun.

On this second beautiful summer day, we enjoyed the weather, one another and funnel cake. At home, they promptly got out the Monopoly game while I made chocolate chip pancakes for dinner (their choice). It was a Monopoly marathon, which they stopped for dinner and then continued later into the night. At some point, they disappeared downstairs to dance and came back up with a newer, fresher plan. Tamar cornered me first, "Can Jessie sleep over? Rachel is going to call her mom."

I knew without even blinking that "yes" was the answer. Rachel's mom called and we both laughed, knowing we had been tag-teamed. When Tamar called her mom, she said, "Jessie and Rachel can sleep over, is that okay?" We didn't have a chance.

And so the day without end continued. Diane drove them to Tamar's house, and it wasn't until noon the next day that I picked them up. They were still having a great time together.

As I thought about their friendship, I realized that there is something so sweet and grounded in their relationship. How lucky they are to have this experience. The girls go to different schools (they attended the same day camp year after year) and have big circles of friends. Yet when they come together, they are still as close as ever. As a woman, I know there is something special about a friend from when you were a toddler that establishes a different sort of friendship. Not better, not worse, just different.

How fortunate to have this experience. My hope is that the friendship continues as they get older. Wouldn't that be lucky for them! In the game of life and in the game of friendship, all three of these girls are winners.

And the Oscar Goes To...

Just one month into middle school, my daughter Jessie, who transitioned extremely well (in fact, much better than her mom), informed me that she would be staying after school for activities in the Drama department.

She popped into the car after school and announced, "I'm auditioning for the school play. Do I have any prior experience? Here! Run my lines with me!" and she was off and running.

Jessie has been dancing since she was three; she only knows life with dance class. Only once in all of her 11 years has she ever expressed any interest in auditioning for or being in a production other than a dance show. When she was six, she auditioned for the Muny.

So I was surprised and happy to hear about these new plans. She was finding her own way in middle school, and it had nothing to do with her brother (who had been there for 3 years and wouldn't be able to tell you where the Drama department is) or her mom. I was all for it. In high school, I was friends with Drama department devotees who were also in the marching band. They were great fun and an amazing group of kids.

Jessie read all the information and rehearsed, rehearsed, rehearsed. In fact, she tried out every part on me and the dog and then would stop and say things like, "isn't this part so me, Mom?" or "do you think this accent works all right?"

The Drama department held auditions on two afternoons, and according to Jessie a lot of students tried out. She had told the drama teacher, Mrs. McCracken, that she would do anything, take any part, big or small, even work on the tech crew. Jessie went to the second day of auditions and reported to me, "I was great! I read with a few different people and I was good." She also had kind words for other would-be-actors, telling me, "I watched all the auditions and Rebecca was funny. We all were laughing." I liked that she had picked up on the supportive atmosphere that I remembered.

Mrs. McCracken posted call-backs online, and Jessie's name was on the long list. Jessie auditioned again at call-backs and once more thought she did well enough to land a part. The teacher would post the cast at 5:00 p.m. the same day.

At 4:59 p.m., Jessie logged on and saw the cast list. I heard her from across the house, over the noise of the clothes dryer and the barking dog. I knew immediately what that meant.

I stopped dinner mid-prep. She was sitting at the computer sobbing. Not crying. Sobbing. Crying huge crocodile tears and shaking. "I can't believe I didn't get a part! I worked so hard," she wailed. I waited while she took another look at the cast list and then beckoned her to let me hold her and hug her. (What other options are there when your child is sobbing?) I held her for a long time before she finally stopped crying. Then she started up again. We moved to the couch and she just fell into me. I rubbed her back and held her, my heart breaking, too.

Oh, if only the teacher could see her now, Jessie would have earned a huge part. In fact Jessie has always been dramatic; when she was much younger and her emotions got the best of her, I would often say, "And the Oscar goes to Jessie for outstanding work in a drama."

When I thought about it, it occurred to me that Jessie (like most kids today) hasn't had much experience with disappointment. Think about it. Our kids say, "I want to play baseball" or "I want to be in a play," and parents do whatever they can to fulfill this wish. We haven't ever been in a situation where one of our kids has worked extremely hard for something and *not* earned whatever it is they were going for.

In all of her 11 years, this was probably Jessie's first meaningful disappointment. Out that night with a group of friends I relayed the story. "What a great life lesson," commented Michelle, the wise one, who has a 19 year old daughter.

As adults we understand that we can try hard and still not achieve what we want. We cry, we move on. We try again. And we learn how important it is to recover from disappointment.

This is the life lesson in our Oscar-earning week for my little thespian. Work hard, give it your best shot, and celebrate when you achieve your goal. And when you don't, try again.

I encouraged Jessie to consider working on the tech crew to learn more about drama. She did, and she enjoyed it tremendously. In addition, the drama teacher got to know her a little better as well.

In January, Jessie again came home filled with excitement, "Mom! It's a musical this time!" She needed no encouragement to audition. This time around Jessie made the chorus (which dances). The teacher sent me an e-mail message: "Jessie did a good audition and earned her spot in the cast. I can tell she worked hard at it! :)" Later, Mrs. McCracken sent me another e-mail: "Jessie is truly giving her best at every rehearsal."

When I asked Jessie about making the musical and how it felt different from the first time, she said, "This time when I made it I was so happy. But I know what it feels like not to make it, so I'm even happier."

Incredibly, in that one year, Jessie had the experience of both trying and failing and trying and succeeding. I only hope that when she finally accepts her Oscar, she remembers me in her speech.

Brothers and Sisters

On a cold Tuesday in late February, I was upstairs trying to get ready to get out of the house for an evening with a lovely group of women. We had rescheduled from a snow day earlier that winter, and I was counting on my husband to be home. On Sunday he informed me that he was leaving town Tuesday morning, returning Wednesday night. I try very hard *not* to leave on school nights. It just doesn't work well for anyone if grownups aren't in the house.

We actually hadn't tried leaving the kids alone for a long while because Jessie didn't like to go to sleep without a goodnight from one of us, and Joe often wasn't particularly helpful.

However, Joe at 14 ½ was clearly old enough to babysit and Jessie at 12 was also doing a little babysitting. They really were old enough to manage one night on their own.

Trying to make it all easy, I worked all day to have lunches packed, house picked up, dinner made, and dishes cleaned up so that the only thing the kids had to do together was eat dinner, put their dishes in the dishwasher (I know I am asking quite a bit here), and finish homework. Joe had pretty much knocked out all his homework, but I knew Jessie would need help studying for the tests and quizzes her teachers were piling on during this week before Sixth-Grade Camp.

She had studied over the weekend, but she needed someone to go over all the material with her one more time. When Joe came home from school I apprised him of the situation. "Sure, I'll help her study. What other homework does she have?"

Every now and then the alien life form surprises me.

These are not close siblings. Often friendly comrades in arms and mostly when I least expect it. This is *not* Donny and Marie by anyone's stretch.

These two simply tolerate one another. With two years, nine months between them, they share no friends or common interests. Their abilities are vastly different, except on the ski slopes. I'm not even sure they like each other.

I remember reading something years ago about how much an older brother can influence how a younger sister feels about herself. This directly ties into her self-esteem, which often concerns me. I caution Joe to be kinder to her than he is. Because he cuts her very little slack, she is one tough cookie. So there are at least some positive consequences to this behavior.

What is interesting is that, when we travel, they get along rather well. They must realize that they only have one another. I would love to plan a big long escape and see how they fare.

It was with much concern and apprehension that I approached Tuesday night when I would leave them alone. I wanted to go out. I needed to stay.

And then a funny thing happened. I was nearly ready to go out when I heard laughter from downstairs.

Laughter?

How was that possible? It was only Joe and Jessie having dinner.

I stopped and listened again.

Definitely laughter. Loud laughter and giggling.

I quietly went halfway down the stairs and listened.

Joe had Jessie's notebook in front of him and he was quizzing her. "No, Washington was not an Imperialistic President!" he laughingly said to her. Jessie was laughing along with him. "I don't know!" she was giggling.

And so it went. And then…gasp!

They cleaned up the kitchen. Together. Not one cross word spoken. Not one punch thrown. Not one towel snapped.

As I said goodnight and gave them last-minute instructions, they were completely fine. "Go!" they both said.

I didn't get one frantic phone call that evening. I was able to enjoy myself (okay, half my brain was at home the entire night) and came home to find the house still standing and two children sleeping soundly. All tucked in for the night.

Wow.

Maybe I should go out more often.

High School Without the Musical

I loved high school. I have wonderful memories of fun, friends, classmates, drill team and yearbook. *We are great, don't say maybe. We're the class of 1980!*

Now my son Joe who is 14, attends the same high school I went to. Only it's not really the same high school. Sure, the building is about the same, and I have clear memories of a few classrooms, the common areas and the field, but the school looks and feels completely different.

The curriculum since 1980 has changed immensely as well. The math that Jessie is doing in sixth grade I was doing in ninth. Joe's core classes seem more like college level than the classes I remember from high school. The expectations from teachers, administrators and society also are much higher and more stringent.

Most kids today take challenging classes from the get-go. I think I knew a few people in high school who took honors classes, and maybe even a few who took college-credit classes, but on the whole, the people I knew in the 80s were not. No, we were much too busy having other kinds of fun.

In the movie "17 Again," Zac Efron's character, Mike, gets the opportunity to go back to high school, and this time he's going to change things. What struck me most about this story was that Mike not only thought he could change things, but in the flashbacks of him in high school, he appeared to be having a good time. Why go back? Why try to change anything? But the underlying message is just that: we can always make it better.

My wish for my kids is to have a great time in high school, the first place where you start figuring out who you are. I would love for Joe to create amazing memories in high school and have no regrets.

Joe seems to be succeeding. I held my breath through those first days (I always worry!) and then realized I had nothing much to be concerned about. Joe has always been the kind of person who assumes responsibility for whatever he needs to take care of and in a timely manner. Yes, he still needs reminders to be nice to his sister, do his laundry, and feed the dog, but when it comes to preparing for a math test, he knows exactly what he has to do.

In fact, his work ethic is quite remarkable. My friend Diane mentioned to me that both her sons used planners to keep themselves on track. I asked Joe about doing that, but he prefers his own method of organization. He just keeps information in his head and then lets me know when a test is coming up or he receives a grade. Since everything is online, he has no trouble keeping tabs on himself. Which he does.

One day after school, right after the close of the first quarter, Joe said to me, "I need to let you know that one of my grades might not be so good." Now in the musical version, this is where my character would break into song, "I'm sure it will all be fine as long as you work hard..." But I can't carry a tune and life is not a musical. If it were, then Joe could have sung to me: "Challenge Math is really, really hard, but I'm doing my best and I like the teacher and he said to keep doing what I'm doing."

Overall, Joe has adjusted quite well to high school. He was on the swim team in the fall and met amazing scholar-athletes who encouraged him in his quest for good grades more than any adult could. Being part of the swim team made him identify and connect with the school.

Joe's teachers are pleased with his efforts, he has made many new friends, and he enjoys going to school each day. He and his friends often attend sporting events (I think it's just to check out the girls) and they always seem to have some plan in progress.

I keep remembering my days in high school and that always brings a smile. Even though Joe doesn't want to hear about my high school days or hear me sing, I think that, for now, Joe is making memories to last his lifetime.

Even if high school isn't a musical.

Everything You Always Wanted to Know About Teenage Boys But Were Afraid to Ask

Purely from a mother's perspective, I have to say that parenting a teenage boy is not like parenting at any other time in our journey together. From having a little boy who adored me and wanted to play catch with me to feeding this man-boy who now inhabits my house (and is much much taller than me), I have been fascinated at every stage.

From the first days of motherhood, most of the friendships I've forged have been with mothers of girls–I call them "girl-moms." But as time went on–and especially now that Joe is in high school–I am finding that the "boy-moms" and I have so much more in common. I get to be the teenage-boy maven because I have a talker! Yes, I am one of the lucky boy-moms: my son actually talks to me. He even tells me (somewhat) interesting things. Well, not always and I'm sure that what he does tell me is often censored. That said I definitely hear about things that the other boy-moms sometimes do not. In typical teenage-boy-mom-mode, we are all happy to share gathered Intel.

Some of what I've learned about teenage boys in general:

1. They are extremely focused. My son Joe can play a video game for hours on end and never once hear me call him to empty the dishwasher, feed the dog, or clean his room. (Can you believe it?)

2. They use creative organization and storage options. Joe often knows exactly where his clean clothes are: his closet, drawers, floor, chair, or laundry basket. I've stopped asking.

3. They *really* eat. And eat and eat and eat. Over winter break, we were skiing with another family that has a son Joe's age. After lunch one day, we headed to the slopes. Within thirty minutes, I found the boys in the pizza place, devouring an enormous pizza. I commented on Joe's big appetite and he replied, "Yeah, I do eat a lot. But not at mealtime. Mostly between mealtimes." Good to know.

4. Teenage boys really like teenage girls and are utterly fascinated by them. Here's what I don't get: I'm a girl. There's no mystery about me. Anything you want to know about being a girl, Joe's sister Jessie and I are happy to explain. Joe apparently prefers to think that teenage girls are a different species from his mom and sister. And, unlike Jessie and me, that other species is intriguing.

5. Teenage boys love to play any game involving (a) a ball or puck and (b) the outdoors, no matter the weather or conditions of the playing surface.

6. Teenage boys smell. You know I'm not even going there. They do. Deal with it.

7. When you rely on teenage boys for information, you must be prepared to (a) change your plans at any minute, (b) confirm with another adult all information learned from your teenager, and (c) understand that the information provided has been filtered through a teenage boy's brain. Adjust accordingly.

8. Teenage boys gain height overnight, usually in middle school, and will take much glee from looking down at their mothers. One summer morning after sixth grade, Joe came down for breakfast and I had to look *up* at him. Somehow his voice also had changed during the night, becoming much deeper. Thus came my uh-oh moment: I was going to have to firmly maintain grownup person status for those times when I would have to enforce our house rules.

9. Teenage boys have a funny, easy sense of humor. It's mostly situational—you have to listen to catch it—but they still like to laugh, joke and be silly. Sometimes they are even ironic.

10. Teenage boys don't "gather" or make plans the same way other humans do. When I first witnessed this I was left open-mouthed and surprised. As time went on I realized that, "we'll figure it out" actually happens in its own teenage boy time frame.

It seems to me that teenage boys are a taller version of that sweet little boy I remember. He still wants a hug goodnight (really) and to tell me all the funny things that happened to him while he was out in the world. The little boy that I adored is still in there, masked by man-boy smell and man-boy interests. But I know the little one I couldn't get enough of is in there. And the adventure continues.

Our House
Is a Very Fine House

Everyday Heroes

"If this isn't love, I don't know what is," Kenny muttered to me over his cell phone one Saturday evening. He was at the grocery store salad bar, trying to make me a salad, and I was at home with two children who weren't feeling well. This made three people at home for a week with flu, including me the previous week.

I laughed. "Oh, I think helping me make it out of bed when I had the flu last week would count, too," I commented.

I began to think of all those little things, all those everyday actions that make Kenny (and many other husbands and fathers) our everyday heroes.

I'll bet I could make a list: How about when Kenny gets up in the middle of the night with a child because I simply don't function at 3:00 a.m.? Or when he works all day, then manages Joe's baseball practice, and then comes home and helps get everyone ready for bed, finally collapsing later to say, "Was there any dinner tonight?" When he is rushing on Monday mornings yet still takes time to load my bike rack and put my bike on the car because I can't lift it? What about the times he takes Jessie to dance class and watches her leap through the air for an hour? Or helps Joe with fourth-grade math that completely confuses me? Does the kids' laundry because I can't get to it? Oh, this is the best. What about when he calls me from Blockbuster to confer on movie choices?

Yep. All those reasons. And more.

Because Kenny is an everyday hero. He's not a firefighter or an astronaut. He doesn't play for the NBA and he's not a corporate CEO. But he is *our* hero.

Because he knows that Joe will eat Go-Gurt but not regular yogurt. Because he knows that Jessie likes to have her hair brushed before she brushes her teeth at bedtime. Because he will walk the dog on those days that I have a million things to do. Because he takes the trash out on Mondays and I never have to ask. Because when I was giving birth to Joe and we were 32 hours into labor, the man never left my side. Because he always tells me my butt doesn't look fat in whatever I am wearing. Because he still buys me string bikinis and expects me to wear them. (Okay, maybe not that last thing!) Because he loves to take walks at night and have neighborhood BBQs. Because he feels that he needs to be at the kids' school conferences. Because he drives carpool on those nights I really want to go to exercise class. Because (and I do believe this is the real reason) he knows where I keep my chocolate stash and never gives it away.

I have noticed, most especially living in this neighborhood, that we are surrounded by everyday heroes. We have dads who come to the bus stop, ride bikes with their kids, invite friends to come play, grow gardens (and let their neighbors share).

Best is that, whenever we are having one of our famous neighborhood BBQs and kids are running around everywhere, the other dads can have a conversation with me (or any other female) regardless of whether my husband is around. Last May, we walked to a neighborhood BBQ, and I was the one who sat down to socialize while Kenny played with the kids. In this little community we are not divided into camps of moms and dads. And while I was sitting, I was able to have a decent discussion with another neighborhood dad about gardening. (I still cannot grow a thing, but I appreciated the vote of confidence.)

Could it be that these dads and their contemporaries closely watched *their* fathers and took all the best there was to create the unique generation of fathers today? Most dads today were in the delivery room, have changed a gazillion diapers, pack lunches, and are very much involved on a day-to-day basis with their offspring. How lucky can we get? Because a great dad just makes everyone's life that much happier. Most of us are better moms because of dads who offer support, love and humor.

But let's not completely sugarcoat this. At this point, Kenny and I have been married 16 years, and believe me, it has not all been a walk on the beach. However, I truly believe that a relationship changes and adapts over time to accommodate everyone. In a relationship of that many years, we have had ups and we have had downs. Yet, here we are, still together. I wish I could put my finger on all the reasons.

An army of fantastic fathers these days willingly spend weekends hiking, biking, camping and swimming with their families. Dads take sick days when nobody else in the household can function. They take frantic calls from their children of any age. They haul home a carload of stuff from Sam's Club. Dads find the right baseball team for their child, and they listen to Cam Jansen for the fiftieth time because their first grader has learned to read. An awful lot of dads can figure out fourth-grade math, and many don't blink an eye when their families have to try every flavor at Ben and Jerry's before deciding what they want. Plenty of dads ski bunny slopes until their kids are ready to move on, play tennis in the heat of summer and teach their kids to drive safely. These are dads that are *here*.

Kenny is one of many amazing fathers who come home every night and announce with love and eagerness, "Hello, I'm home."

Island Time

On a trip to the mountains in Colorado over Spring Break, I marveled at how skiers, like islanders, have their own clocks. What matters to skiers is not real time, but when the mountain opens and the ski lifts begin their ascent. Like islanders the skiers' internal clocks mandate when they ski (or surf), eat and finally, succumb to complete exhaustion.

Kids are a lot like this. They have no sense of time. They just want to do what they want to do when they want to do it. There's something to be said for living life according to your internal clock or with a skiers or surfers mentality. Mountain Time or Island Time might be a state of mind, but is the perfect place for a frustrated beach girl to live.

I would love to live my life here, now, on Island Time. Since I believe it is internal, I have some work to do. Kenny always laughs when I say, "I am so busy!" "You are the busiest person I know," he often comments when he asks my plans for the day.

Yes, I am busy. But who isn't?

Of course the other part of this–and I wonder if anyone out there feels the same way–it takes me so much longer to run errands these days. I am not sure if it's me (oh no! I am turning into my Grandma Sally who could make An Event out of errand running!) or if there is just so much more to do now to keep a family in tip-top shape.

Running errands takes huge bites out of my time…sometimes the entire afternoon is gone–for one errand.

And I don't even *like* to run errands!

Whenever we go on vacation, I try not to do my regular, boring activities. I take time off from the gym and walk on the beach. I don't shave my legs every day; every other is fine. If I can get away without cooking, doing laundry and cleaning, I am certainly going to try.

Yet at the moment of reentry (my friend Patti's term for returning to real life from a vacation or trip), my mind starts organizing. Who needs to be where when? What is on the calendar? What commitments do we have?

I wonder what my life would be like if I really lived on Island Time. And why not start in the summer when living is easy, when we don't have plans, the sun is out, the pool is open…

Yeah, great thought.

Here's what really happens. My kids like to go to camp, which means making lunches, doing laundry, carpooling. You know—all the same activities that we all do all the time. Add in baseball practices and games as well as swim lessons and the entire summer starts to look and feel like the very busy school year.

Something has to give.

I come up with my usual ideas and pitch them to Kenny.

"Let's take all the money we spend on camp and go to the island for the summer." That's my usual opening.

"Um, what island would you be thinking of?" he asks very innocently. "We live in the midwest."

"Oh, that! How about the Cape?" I try another tactic. We had spent one of our best vacations ever on Cape Cod with friends from Boston. While we were there, I met quite a few families who had inherited Cape houses from grandparents. They had spent their summers "on the Cape," and now their kids were doing the same thing. They swam in the ocean, traveled on the bike path and just hung out all summer.

I could do that.

"Well, that sounds really good for you, but I can't take the summer off." It's the same argument Kenny uses each time I bring this up.

"How about you come with us the first week and I stay for a few weeks with the kids and then you come up the last week?" I try again.

"Yeah, I don't think so," is his usual response.

What would be so terrible about this? We could live on Island Time where the living is easy and comfortable. Do what you what when you want. No demands (who *am* I kidding?), just hanging out enjoying the summer. Remember that great Diane Lane movie, *Walk on the Moon?* She had an amazing summer "on the beach." This, of course, is where my logic begins to break down.

Oh, how I would love to live on Island Time all day every day. I wonder how to achieve this state of mind, landlocked as I am in the middle of the country. There just has to be a way. There has to be a way to slow down, enjoy a stress-free life, and not be so calendar dependent.

When I figure it out, I'll let you know. For now, I've got my sunscreen, a good book and the kids…I'm heading to the beach.

A Day at the Beach

There is no place I would rather be than the beach. No two ways about it. If I had the opportunity I would live *on* the beach. I would move in a nano-second. In fact, every once in a while, when things get out of hand at home and the stress level is chocolate-worthy I pull out my fall-back suggestion:

"Want to sell everything and go live in a tiki hut on the beach?"

By now my family just humors me. They think I am kidding.

Last August we took a week-long vacation to the beach, traveling in an RV. Since I am currently land-locked I lobby for beach vacations whenever possible. The drive was long (though not hard), giving me a lot of time to think about how nice it would be to live on the beach, and all the things a family might learn by living there. I thought maybe if I explained myself my family would finally take me seriously…and we could investigate that tikki hut.

While thinking about this, it occurred to me that even if we never moved there, after all these RV trips I knew a thing or two about insuring an amazing trip for everyone. Here are some of my thoughts:

If at all possible, take a detour to see old friends. So here we are traveling along on Friday night and Kenny asks me to confirm our itinerary. We are at a rest stop, having dinner somewhere outside of Memphis, and I open the map. Glancing at the map, I suddenly notice the name of the town where my friend Susan has lived for about 6 years. Can it be possible that we are actually this close without a plan? I wonder if Susan and her family are even home. We are too close not to try to contact them. I went into action with my cell phone and was able to track her down through a network of mutual friends. And- we ended up pulling into her driveway at 11:00 pm. This could not have worked out better if we had tried to plan it! It was such fun to catch up, have breakfast with Susan's family and finally see her house.

Travel with music. It becomes the soundtrack of your trip. My brilliant kids downloaded all our CDs to an iPod. Then Kenny found an adapter that let us play the iPod through the RV's sound system. At times, we all sang along, and often I heard Kenny explaining to the kids who John Denver or R.E.M. were. "Country Roads," songs from "High School Musical," and "Teach Your Children" were our favorites.

If you get turned around, get yourself UN-turned around. Kenny and I are at our absolute *best* when we travel. If only we could travel all the time, our lives would be so uncomplicated and happy. Kenny doesn't like to use trip plans from the Auto Club; he prefers to roam wherever the road takes us, as long as we eventually get to our destination. Many times he would consult the map or spot a road sign and ask, "will this work?" And nine times out of ten, it sure does. There are however, those occasions when I throw down the map in frustration because we are...lost.

Get as CLOSE to the beach as possible. In our many travels by RV, we have found glorious campgrounds *right on* a beach. There is something so special about waking up to the sound of the waves, the sight of the shoreline, and the smell of saltwater. On our most recent trip to Sandestin, Florida, we could see the ocean from the windows of the RV. Yes, there is sand *everywhere*, but the ocean is spectacular in the early morning as the sun comes up. And the sunsets? There are no words for a beach sunset. Just a really-good-that-we-did-this-feeling.

Take a good book, or two, or three. I confess: I am a slug when it comes to the beach. I like playing in the water and jumping waves, but even more, I adore just lounging in my beach chair, following the sun, and reading a really good book. On our first day at the beach

I stayed put over 7 hours. I alternated reading and playing with the kids, but I had no desire to move from my spot on the beach. I was in heaven. Plus, I was reading an amazing book.

Yes, Virginia, there *is* wildlife in the ocean. Even where we swim. Okay, I like the ocean, but ummm, I do *not* like to be bothered by the critters. Or, if they do get close, I don't want to know about it. Of course I love wildlife. I just don't want them to touch me. This particular beach had more fish in the surf than I can remember. Great, super. The kids loved snorkeling to check them out. But this just made me more aware that we are not alone. (Shiver.)

Be creative with transportation. The RV we now travel in is a 35-footer, and towing a car makes it even longer. Instead, we bring our bikes. And while I do not like riding on roads, we have been lucky in finding bike trails and sidewalks that ultimately lead us to vegetable stands and fish markets. The kids love riding to the grocery store. It makes them feel as though we are living in a totally different world.

Even camping, chocolate is a must. Before we left, I stocked up on fun, interesting treats that we might not have at home so that the kids would think of these as RV specialties. More than anything else- never underestimate the power of Nutella on graham crackers.

There is no place like home. The trip last summer was one of our best. All the pieces fell into the right place, and everyone had a good time. The dog loved playing in the ocean, the kids loved camping, and Kenny and I loved that our family was able to spend some low-key, quality time together in the great outdoors. Yet, when we pulled into our neighborhood and saw our house, we let out a collective sigh. We were home. Safe and sound. Happy to see our own little tiki hut in the middle of suburbia.

The Brady Bunch

Last November, I found "The Brady Bunch" on Channel 13 at 8:00 p.m. weeknights. Our lives haven't been the same since.

"Come on, you guys, watch this it's a great show," I said on the first night that Joe, Jessie and I cuddled up to watch it. Kenny was out of town and I was out of energy.

Since then, "The Brady Bunch" has become a nightly ritual for us. Everyone gets everything done homework, lunches, dinner dishes, showers, everything and we all meet up for the Brady's.

I am *the* biggest "Brady Bunch" geek ever! Ask my sister. I know *every* episode, all the dialogue, every story line. I have read all the books, seen the movies and the stage show (here and in D.C.), and even dragged my sister many years ago to meet Maureen McCormack ("Marcia," for all you non-watchers) at a Best Buy.

My sister will tell you that I wanted to *be* Marcia Brady. I wanted that hair, those sisters and brothers, that life. That simple, simple life, with Alice always in the kitchen making dinner and Mom and Dad always patiently listening or helping to solve any of life's problems. No problem was too big or too small for the Bradys. And when life got really tough, they either reenacted the crime or they went to the Grand Canyon.

When life gets to be too tough for me, too complex, too full of dishwashers, I turn to the Bradys. It took two shows for my kids to get hooked, and just a week's worth of shows for Jessie to start singing the theme song. All the Bradys' problems can be happily solved in 22 minutes. Even when someone is crabby, by show's end, they have talked it through and decided to go to the pizza parlor together.

Wouldn't that be something, if we could solve all our problems in about 22 minutes? And how about that pizza parlor? No low-carb dieting going on back then.

Nothing changes at the Bradys'. The living room still looks the same. The stairs look the same. Even the kids' bedrooms and bathroom look the same. When we built this house I said, "Let's build a 'Brady Bunch' bathroom," and everyone knew what I was talking about!

It's always calm at the Bradys'. And warm and inviting. And Alice has pie.

Boy, what I wouldn't give to have an Alice come live with us! Seriously, another adult (and I use that term lightly) to make lunches; make *any* kind of meal and wow! think of the child care options. I could run out at any time and know the kids were well taken care of. And of course there's the aspect of having somebody living here just to hang out with. Really groovy.

So it should have come as no surprise to me when, after a particularly busy, crazy week, Kenny had a really far-out idea.

"You know, I know the Bradys are just a show, and we could never be as happy as they are all the time, but we could try a little bit harder at our house," he said. I had to smile because lately in our house, everything was Brady. (And what was he talking about the Bradys not being "real"?)

I laughed when Kenny compared our chaotic, messy life and our house to the Bradys'. I don't remember Carol Brady ever losing an important piece of paper as a result of her creative filing. I don't ever remember Mike Brady throwing his hands up and saying, "There are so many piles in this house, how do you even know where anything is?"

Life is definitely busier, faster and crazier today than when the Bradys were in their heyday.

But that doesn't mean that I can't look at the Bradys and find the positive messages there: family first; don't throw balls in the house; oh, my nose; and of course, the *best* message ever: Marcia, Marcia, Marcia. In our messy, chaotic, loud house there is always room for the Bradys.

Far out, man.

Cash for Clunkers

I have never been overly attached to things. I like my family pictures and my clothes (and my house), but I could easily walk away from everything if someone said, "Beach House It's yours! Go now!"

So, when Kenny said, "I think we need to get a new car," I hesitated.

The reason the subject even came up was that our car wouldn't pass inspection without thousands of dollars worth of work. In the past, if the car needed work I was the one who jokingly said, "Oh, let's just get a new one." For some reason it didn't occur to me that that would one day happen.

Anyone who knows Kenny (and let me just say here, he is a *great* guy), they know that it takes him three months to make a decision. About anything. And I'm just the opposite. We have a great partnership.

As good, upstanding citizens, we took our car to the dealer for inspection in late July, and by August 1, Kenny had bought a new car. This is monumental. This is amazing. Seriously, I still can't get the guy to make up his mind about dinner.

Now I have to give up my car. Me, the girl who isn't attached to things.

This *thing*, however, has been with me as long as Jessie has. It carried my two babies around and kept my toddlers safe. This car saw Joe go off to preschool and now picks him up from middle school. It has carried numerous kids over the last decade, playing "Sweet or Sour" from the reverse-facing back seat. Sometimes I would have five little girls in the car all chattering away. A few times I had five very large boys in there.

I love this car. I love the way it looks, sounds and feels. It's comfortable, like an old blanket. It feels so heavy and safe and…mine.

What is worse, though, is all the great bumper stickers covering the back bumper. (can you imagine that conversation with Mr. Practical?) There's the Ron Jon Surf Shop that I picked up when we were there with the kids. The Big Sur sticker from the most amazing road trip down the Pacific Coast Highway. We stayed in Big Sur overnight and then headed down the coast to go out on a whale watch in Monterey. There is a bumper sticker from The Great Smoky Mountains, where we went hiking one spring break—one of our best RV trips, ever. Everyone loved that adventure.

I know it sounds silly, but I really like that my car reflects where I've been, where I'm going and who I am. Seriously, bumper stickers do say all that to me. Of course the fact that I happen to be driving a gas-guzzling SUV bothered me, but those bumper stickers—boy that really reflected who I was. And wouldn't you know that Mr. Practical has asked me to *not* put any bumper stickers on a new car.

Ironically, once we had made the decision to trade in the car (for a hybrid that, I swear, runs on popcorn oil); it began to make even more mysterious noises, as if it were on its last legs. Suddenly, this car knew that its days of being a family car were numbered, so why not go out big, noisy, and with attitude? Over the course of a few days, the noises grew louder and more disturbing: we didn't think the car was going to make it onto the lot. After all, it was 10 years old, with 148,000 miles.

Now that we had decided to "go green," I was curious what happened to the clunkers that were traded in. The goal was to remove these cars from the road, so chances were the outcome wasn't going to be good. Apparently, they take all they can from the old vehicles and use the parts. Then they squash the car (gasp) and use it to make a refrigerator or some other useful thing. This kind of recycling should actually make me feel better about what we are doing.

But I really will miss this car. It might have another life as a refrigerator, oven, or garage door. Its parts might go to a million other places and repair a zillion other appliances. That's great for the environment, for our planet.

As for my car well, now that car exists only in my memories.

Thanks for the ride.

One More Thing

Like the straw the broke the camel's back, I knew that whatever would eventually reduce me to tears would be no big deal. It would be something simple, that in the best of times, I would laugh off.

Our spring has been a little hectic.

We decided to build a rec room in our basement, with new floors and walls and a bathroom, so that, as the kids got older, they would have their own space. Our basement was actually a kid haven, with cement walls and floors and old furniture that couldn't be hurt. In cold weather Jessie and her friends would happily skate down there for hours.

I am not sure what possessed me to think that a little remodeling would make it all that much better. But, as usual, I jumped in with both feet and we began construction. We had been given an estimate of 6 to 8 weeks to completion. As I sit here now, it has been 16 weeks and there is no end in sight.

In the middle of all of this, we are also preparing Joe for his thirteenth birthday and everything that goes along with that. And of course we're keeping up with everyone's homework, baseball and softball schedules, dance rehearsals and friends. There is a lot going on.

So I wasn't prepared when our veterinarian advised us to see a veterinary surgeon because Crosby was limping. Crosby is a four-year-old, 90-pounds-of-pure-puppy German Shepherd who thinks she is a lap dog. She is smart, sweet, and mischievous. "Marley" has nothing on her.

Crosby needed surgery to rebuild her knee. In the end our dog's knee would be bionic. She would run faster, jump higher and chase more efficiently. The surgery itself was no big deal. It was the required recuperation time that was going to test me to my limits.

When outside, she had to be on a leash at all times. She was not allowed to go up or down steps or hills. No jumping, playing, or sliding and no wood floors.

Our lives changed in a matter of days. We told the kids that all of us would have to step up and help take care of Crosby. And, they have, with very little complaining.

But Crosby herself doesn't like to be restrained or limited and after pulling her staples out for the third time, the vet advised us to sedate her to "take the edge off." Um, could you sedate me, too?

As life goes, you just deal with what you are given. Lemons? No problem—we'll make lemonade.

When we had first learned that Crosby needed surgery, Kenny said, "There's no choice. She's a member of the family. This is where we are right now." I liked the way he said that and repeated his words to the kids. I wanted them to know that, as a family, we would take care of Crosby to the best of our ability. Not only is that just in our nature, but little eyes are watching Mom and Dad. And though I hate to admit it, little eyes are judging me and my every move.

As we changed our lives to accommodate Crosby's needs, I realized that this was a perfect learning opportunity for our kids, a great time to teach them how to deal with those unexpected things that life throws at you.

One friend in particular said something that gave me pause. "Have a plan toward something. Don't get stuck running in circles." So I did just that. I made a plan with Kenny and the kids and felt much calmer and more in control. Maybe I just got used to the changes. Whatever the case, I managed to handle each crisis one at a time and in a calm, reasonable manner.

When the dishwasher leaked all over the kitchen floor one night, I was composed. When the car kept making that horrible clunking noise, I remained calm. (Honestly, I couldn't believe it. Aren't we doing everything in our power to make sure that everyone is well taken care of? Aren't we being fiscally responsible? Aren't we going green?) And when I realized how much my life was about to be considerably altered, I stayed cool: Crosby had only about a three-hour window each day when she could be left alone.

Sigh.

One evening, Kenny commented, "You're handling this all really well."

What else could I do? Sit down and cry? Run away to a beach hut? Not deal with it?

Hey, those aren't bad ideas. Does anyone have any chocolate?

Puppy Love

For the first time in nine years, I will be alone all day. For six weeks this summer, both my children will be going to day camp at the same place and at the same time. I will drop them both off in the morning and return 6 hours later. I will be on my own. Sigh. Bliss. Freedom.

So, what do we decide to do?

Get a puppy.

It's not like I was looking for something to do. I have a list. And I certainly did not need someone else to take care of. Believe me, I have my hands full already.

It's not like I thought, "oh no! now what?!!!"

There just is no perfect time to have a baby or adopt a puppy.

When Kenny and I were first together, we had a puppy that grew into the worlds' best dog. As a 6-week-old puppy, Starr howled each night to the point of driving me to tears. She decimated the alarm clock we had given her to imitate the sound of her mother's heart when the puppies were in the womb, and she destroyed the teddy bear we gave her to cuddle up with. She did keep that teddy bear, though, and would often play with it. She was so funny. A huge dog carrying around a stuffed pink teddy bear with no face.

Starr was a German Shepherd and we thought the most amazing dog. She was an alpha female and while I am pretty sure that she knew she was a dog, I often think that she thought she was human, and leader of our pack. As a puppy, she destroyed everything. She ate through the floor, chewed on corners of drawers and knocked pictures off the walls to eat the frames. As she grew older, however, she calmed down. Starr was *not* allowed on the furniture, and that is why most mornings we woke up and found a 70-pound German Shepherd asleep between us. She always greeted me by wagging that huge tail that thumped on the bed.

Once, when Starr was a puppy, she ate a bottle of ibuprofen and a bottle of glue. Apparently, ibuprofen is lethal to dogs. When I arrived home to find her eyes glazed and unsteady, I rushed her to the vet in pouring rain. I stayed with her as they pumped her stomach and hooked her up to IVs. I did what came naturally to me: I talked to her. When I stopped, the nurses encouraged me to continue, commenting, "This is amazing. Her heart rate went up as you were talking." I stayed beside her at home while she slept, hooked up to an IV all night.

Starr was 7 years old when we brought Joe home. She knew I was pregnant. I don't know how, but she did. She became even more protective of me. She put herself between me and anyone else. We discussed and researched what to do when you bring a baby into a house with a dog. Kenny dutifully brought home a blanket from the hospital the day before Joe and I came home. When we arrived home, we left Joe in his car seat and put him down. I held my breath as we both sat on the ground and watched as Starr sniffed and licked him. (Yes, I really let her do that on their first introduction!)

Joe and Starr took to each other immediately. If Starr had been a two-person dog, she apparently had been waiting her whole life to have a kid of her own. She loved Joe. And Joe could spend lots of time looking at her. He was never startled when she barked. Whenever he could, he would get handfuls of fur. Joe's very first word was "Starr."

While I was pregnant with Jessie, Starr got very sick and died quickly. The gap she left in our family was huge. We felt an intense loss. I couldn't imagine any other dog ever coming close to being what Starr had been to us.

We knew that this was not the time to get a puppy. I was going to have a new baby. Then we moved to a new house. And then Jessie needed speech therapy. There just was never a good time to get a puppy. But last spring, I started looking.

A few months ago, the kids brought up the puppy subject again.

"What do you think?" I asked Kenny. I was more than up for it. I really liked having a dog in the family.

"Let's do the whole thing!" was Kenny's reply. I wondered if that meant the white picket fence, too?

Within days we found puppies on a farm with two females that had 18 puppies between them, and within hours we decided to get one.

And so, for the first time in 9 years, my opportunity of being alone? My chance to not have to worry about noon drop-offs? My big escape into the world of being gone all day long with girlfriends and errands?

Well, I keep thinking to myself…freedom is just another word for nothing left to lose and I honestly I didn't think freedom is all that its cracked up to be. How could I fore-go more sleepless nights and puppy training? There were a million reasons *not* to get a puppy. There were two really good ones: Joe and Jessie

Say hello to Crosby Starr, the newest member of our household.

Crosby Starr is now a fully grown, 6-year-old German Shepherd, and I couldn't live without her. She has a playful personality and is so much more connected to our family than I would have imagined. She treats Joe like a littermate, rolling around and wrestling with him. We often find the two of them asleep together on his bed at night. Jessie and Crosby have a unique relationship; Jessie has a gift with animals and Crosby never tests her.

What a good decision it was to bring a dog into our world. I say that now, after I've survived her puppyhood. This one was even more challenging than the first. She ate the window sills on all the front windows. She gave herself a double infection by removing the stitches from her spaying. And after visiting with all the vets in the group practice, Crosby decided that she didn't like any vets at all. She must be double muzzled for a routine office visit.

I think that I've spent more time with Crosby because she is the dog we've had with the kids. I often talk with her when we are in the house alone. In fact, I didn't realize that I also ask her questions. "Hope you're not expecting a reply," my husband said the first time he observed this.

There is no perfect time for a baby or a dog and yet somehow we found the perfect time in our lives to add to our family. Crosby is a people dog and willingly goes hiking, walking or playing anytime. She imagines herself one of the kids and can often be found outside when they are. Be prepared. If you come to visit, she will assume you are there for her. Having a dog changed our lives…for the better.

Our pack wouldn't be complete without her.

Counting Shoes

When *I* was in high school, my friend Carolyn had the best basement to hang out in. Her grandmother lived with her family, so her dad had constructed an entire house downstairs, complete with kitchen and bathroom. They had left one room sort of "undone"; that's where we had our sleepovers. Carolyn was an only child, a status that she handled with grace and selflessness. Her house was always open to everyone. Anyone could sleep over any time, and her parents were incredibly generous.

Her mom used to say, "I know how many kids are here by counting shoes," because we all left our shoes by the basement door.

About a week before the last Friday night in October, our son Joe, who is 13 and in eighth grade, asked, "Is it okay if I have people over Friday night after the football game?" It was such a charming way of putting the request to me: What he really was asking was, "Can I have a boy-girl party in our basement?"

Kenny and I had to be somewhere until about 9:00 p.m., but we gave the okay for the get-together after that, as long as one of us was here. Kenny told Joe that he was responsible for cleaning up the basement by Thursday to have people over on Friday.

I asked Joe what I could get him for his party. He replied, "soda, chips," and I knew right away that I could do better than that. I picked up four kinds of chips, cookies, M&Ms (what kind of kid doesn't love a huge bowl of M&Ms?), and three kinds of soft drinks. The soda was what really got the kids excited. "I wish I was having a party," Jessie commented. All because of soda? I asked myself. I had a feeling it was the freedom to do whatever they wanted in a space created just for kids.

On Friday night after the football game, carloads of kids began to be dropped off at our house. We asked Joe to let everyone in through the front door, so that Kenny and I could greet the kids as they came in. I introduced myself to each person and asked who they were if I didn't know them. I did know all but two or three. My ulterior motive, of course, was to have the kids know we were here in case they needed anything and that *we were here.*

I didn't ask one person to take their shoes off. Yet, as they walked in, one after another threw their shoes in a big pile by the basement door. I thought of Carolyn's mom saying she always knew how many were in her house by counting shoes, and smiled. Had I really come that far so fast?

Apparently, the kids had a good time. We heard them singing, talking and laughing (who knew they could be so loud?). They all filed upstairs about 11:00 p.m. and went outside to play basketball, both boys and girls. It was a nice night, so I thought it was okay as long as they weren't too loud (which they weren't). I just didn't want them running through the neighborhood (which they didn't).

Kenny and I were still barely awake by midnight when the kids started leaving. By 12:20, they were all safely at home, and our son was asleep in his bed.

The next morning, when we asked Joe about his party, he said, "It was the best ever. Our basement is perfect for parties!"

Apparently, our basement, like Carolyn's basement, is perfect without shoes. The party was a success and our son felt good about the party he had thrown. I think deep-down I was most happy that our home was open and welcoming to Joe and his friends. Often I find piles of shoes near the basement door and I know that Joe and his friends are in the "man-cave" playing video games, watching movies or just hanging out. As a parent I am so happy I can provide this space for him and his friends. I am now counting girl shoes; as Jessie has begun making claim to the basement and all the fun it has to offer.

When I find myself counting shoes I feel happy and glad that I can. I always hoped to have a house that was open and generous and full of fun. I often think of Carolyn and her parents whenever I find myself counting shoes and think that's how they must have felt.

The Anniversary Gift

In May 2010, Kenny and I celebrated our twentieth anniversary. In the movie version of my life, we would have been on a beach in Greece or eating tomatoes and mozzarella in Spain.

In the real-life version of my life, we were here in suburbia, shuffling kids and dealing with household logistics. Just living life, trying to figure out how to be all the places we needed to be, including baseball practice and a fifth-grade orchestra concert.

We are an old, boring, married couple.

A few days before our anniversary, which fell on a Thursday, Kenny inquired what my plans were. I didn't have any, but asked if he wanted to take the afternoon off. I had planned to meet up with a friend in the morning, never thinking I should "X" out the day.

As it happened, Kenny was able to take the entire day off, so I rescheduled with my friend and shuffled other activities. On Wednesday, Kenny asked whether I had any plans or if he should make them.

Hmmm. I am constantly making all the plans for everyone. Even when I'm not involved, it seems that I am making plans.

"Oh, please! Make the plans," I replied.

"Do you have any requests? What about hiking or lunch?"

"Let's go biking!" Any chance I get, I prefer biking.

Kenny agreed to make all the arrangements. After sleeping in on a school morning, we awoke at 7:30 a.m. to a torrential downpour. We are outdoor people; however, any outdoor plans were not going to happen today.

We regrouped and decided to get a couples massage (*so* not my idea), have lunch and see a movie.

Having lunch out on a Thursday was decadent, as was the massage. They were both wonderful treats, and I am glad that I went with the plan. After the massages, we saw "Date Night," which was a perfect movie to see on our anniversary, especially because throughout the movie, Steve Carrell and Tina Fey kept calling themselves "an old, boring, married couple." Near the end, Steve's and Tina's characters realized that there was glory in being an old, boring, married couple.

When we got home, we realized that we needed to pick Joe up from Eighth-Grade Day at Six Flags and then get Jessie, our fifth-grader, to her orchestra concert.

When we first realized that Jessie's final concert fell on our anniversary, we both sort of said, "nice way to spend our anniversary." At dinner that evening, Jessie said, "I think I want you to videotape tonight. And get every word everyone says."

At the orchestra concert, the fourth grade played first, and then the fifth grade performed. They performed three songs and then the teacher, Ms. A., announced, "We have a special dedication tonight," and she turned the microphone over to Jessie.

"Mom and Dad, our next song is "Canon in D," which is usually played at weddings. Since it's your twentieth anniversary, I want to dedicate it to you. Happy Anniversary!" and with that, everyone clapped, she sat down, the orchestra played, and I couldn't stop smiling.

Wow. What an amazing gift.

After the concert, we gave Jessie a big hug. She said that she had come up with the idea a few days before and asked the teacher if it was okay. She said that everyone in the fifth-grade orchestra had been in on the secret and that she had been nervous and jittery all day. How lucky Jessie was to have such a supportive teacher and class!

"What a beautiful anniversary gift," I said to Jessie, Mrs. B. (a friend and the accompanist), and Ms. A.

"I'm sure this is just where you wanted to spend your anniversary," Ms. A. replied.

"You know, I can't think of anyplace I would rather be," I said and I meant it. Sometimes it's hard to remember the little moments that make a life, but I know I will remember this anniversary and the little girl who made it so very special.

Hmmm. The beach in Greece, mozzarella and tomatoes in Spain, or the fifth-grade orchestra concert with our 11-year-old daughter giving a special dedication for our anniversary?

No choice. Hands down. Boring, old, married couple. Steve and Tina have nothing on us.

Postcards from My Uncle

When I was growing up, wherever in the world my Uncle Steve was, he sent postcards. He traveled extensively and my sister Staci and I always knew we could count on getting cards from him. They always depicted the locale on the front and he usually wrote a simple message to us on the back.

Now I wish I had had the foresight to keep those postcards. Like Buffy Davis, who had her Uncle Bill on that great 60s television show "Family Affair," I too had an amazing uncle.

I was born during Steve's senior year in high school; my dad was six years older than him. My claim to fame is that I was the first grandchild born on both sides of the family.

Uncle Steve embraced the ideals of the 60s, like totally, man. He has never stopped dressing like the hippie he became. After attending Princeton, he made his way to Antioch College and then to Chicago for one of his first graduate degrees. He eventually ended up in San Francisco–truly, the perfect place for him–writing books and teaching computer art. Although I've asked over and over, not one of his books has ever been dedicated to me. Luckily, Uncle Steve never stopped embracing the ideals of the flower power generation, either. Not only did he look like he had just stepped out of a time warp, he had far-reaching ideals about everything–art, politics, religion, raising kids. He was well read and could converse on any topic.

Ironically, when he came to stay with us he loved watching cable television, because being a hippie; he wouldn't have it in his house. When I visited him I asked, "can you even get TV without it?" "Yes" is the answer, as we watched a Joan Baez special on PBS. And wow, while we watched the program, Uncle Steve and Aunt Cathy mentioned that they had actually seen Joan perform in Muir Woods, the famous redwood forest just outside San Francisco.

I have Uncle Steve to thank for so many things. First, my name. Apparently, in high school Steve was dating Pamela Stedmond, and when my mom met her she not only thought Pamela was beautiful, but so was her name. I ask you, how many Pamelas are running around? Couldn't he have been dating a Tricia or a Zoe? Here I am, 48 years later, with this name. Recently Steve went to his fortieth high school reunion and there she was-Pamela Stedmond in all her glory. "Did you tell her I was named after her?" I asked excitedly. He laughed.

I was about 5 or 6 when my sister and I were flower girls in his first wedding. I have very clear memories of wearing a beautiful yellow mini-dress and throwing flower petals with my sister in a lovely back yard. I was 28 when my sister and I were in Uncle Steve's second wedding, this one in Stern Grove in San Francisco. We were no longer flower girls, although it still felt like it.

When I was a junior in college, my dad and uncle drove me to school in what turned out to be a lively road trip. The two of them together laughed the entire way and I learned more about their childhoods and my grandparents. They were evidently raised by two sets of entirely different parents (both of which were my grandparents.) Hmmm.

It was also Uncle Steve's idea that my sister and I travel together. In March 1989, we visited him in San Francisco. We were completely fascinated by the city and by his wild purple bathroom, where, if you angled yourself just the right way, you could see the Golden Gate Bridge while you shampooed.

Time and again during my life, Uncle Steve has stepped in as a second dad to me. He was great to bounce ideas off of about career choices and college. He was the one who walked me down the aisle at my wedding (for the first time in his life wearing a tux and I have the pictures to prove it). Recently, my son Joe who is 14, commented to me, "For all purposes, Uncle Steve is like my grandpa." A young, hippie grandpa.

I consider myself fortunate to have been my dad's daughter and Uncle Steve's niece. Together, they leave me with a legacy of boundless ideas, funny stories and pride in my Wilson-ness. They were and are Wilson through and through and as the universe would have it... Every now and then I see a little Wilson peeking through when I watch my kids.

Sadly, this past January my Uncle Steve lost his brave fight with cancer. Many days, I wish I could send a postcard to Uncle Steve. It would say:

"Wish you were here."

I've Got All My Sisters with Me

The Goddess Rules. Part 2

This past summer, I read the most hilarious book, titled (don't laugh) *The Goddess Rules*. Trust me; the book was much better than the title. The premise was two women, one older and one younger, spending the summer together and teaching one another rules to live by…or break, depending on which chapter you may be reading.

It made me think about a few of my girlfriends and the wisdom that they have shared with me. Here are their Goddess Rules for life.

With every day, you will feel better. -Patti

We bonded over Daniel Day Lewis in *The Last of the Mohicans*. We ended up in London one summer together and traveled to Ireland to search out DDL. (We didn't find him.) When I had Joe, she came to visit me in the hospital and said, "You will feel better with each day," and she was right. When I had Jessie, she came to my house and did my laundry. Patti is wise beyond even what she knows. And you will always have fun when you are with Patti–promise.

Always keep an emergency $20 in your wallet. -Grandma Sally

I am not sure that she really said this, but her philosophy was similar: Make sure you have a backup plan.

Don't worry, be happy. -Joanie

It may sound trite, but my friend Joanie really lives her life this way. When she is worried, she lets you know. For the most part, she lives her life with a smile and a hearty laugh, which encourages you to just sit back and relax with her. It's that easy.

If it's not fun, don't do it, Mommy. -Jessie

This past year, I decided to take a class at the university. It was not any fun, and each week I would grouse about how much I didn't want to do the work. With those big blue eyes and earnest face, Jessie turned to me one morning and said, "If it's not fun, Mom, don't do it." She is indeed her mother's daughter.

My evenings are for my family. -Jenny

Jenny doesn't leave her house at night. And please don't even *think* of calling her after 9:00 p.m. Yet, she accomplishes more in one day than I do in a week.

Yes, I will come with you for some chocolate. -Staci

My sister, Staci, is one of those awe-inspiring women who seem to have all the balls—family, work, household, fun—in the air at the same time. She is a truly grounded person, and all her choices come from there. She is *the* nicest person I know. And she never says "no" when I suggest that we go find some chocolate.

Let's mobilize the sisters, and/or Let's GO! -Cheryl and Tami

If you ever want to get anything done, call Cheryl. She has this way of getting things accomplished not just efficiently but with style. And the way Tami navigates the world is awe-inspiring. Not sure how we did it, but once in New York, we actually found the Manolo store. If you ever want to simply *go* anywhere, call Cheryl and Tami. They will go anywhere at any time.

Stand for what and who you believe in. -Karen

My friend Karen is the most loyal person I know. She stands firm about what and whom she believes in. Having Karen on your side is like starting out on the winning team. And what's even better is that she lets you know it.

Yes, we will order dessert. -Playgroup Moms

When we go to dinner, I always check out dessert first. Seriously, this group always encourages dessert. Even if they don't want it, they will gladly sit and chat while dessert is ordered. You won't find a more supportive or adventurous group of friends anywhere. They will try anything....and laugh about it.

Let's dance! -Jodi and Abby

If you ever need girlfriends who are willing to go out and dance to the 80s (actually, they will dance to anything), call these two. They are always up for a night of dancing with their girlfriends. And it's always a blast.

You know what you are doing. -Susan

We've known each other since we were three. We've seen the good, the bad and the high-school crushes. Need I say more?

Of course you can be the sixth sister. -Mimi

My friend Mimi is one of five sisters. Yet, whenever I am around them, they always make me feel like a sister. It's always nice to be included.

Skinny Margaritas for the table. -Gym Friends

One morning before we even started exercising, all of us felt as if a margarita was the perfect thing after a "strictly strength" class. It was.

Find the happy. -Cutlan

It's there-find it. Stay with it. Life's too short not to.

Keep your feet relaxed. -Karen, the Dance Instructor

I think she is just so cool. Karen teaches in a way that exudes patience and confidence. I love to be in her class to learn and listen. And you should see her triple-time step.

Blonde streaks looks good on anybody. -Linda

This is just an example of the way in which Linda lives her life. She just goes for it each and every day. She is incredibly intelligent and has amazing feminist ideas. Today is the day. Right now. Live.

I know without a shadow of a doubt that there is a Goddess in each of us. Here are my Goddess rules for an adventurous, fun life:

Have fun.
Make new friends.
Keep old friends.
See the world.
Eat chocolate.
Get to the beach as much as possible.
Wave goodbye.
Be outdoors whenever you can.
Live, love, laugh.
Keep track of your money.
Ride the waves.
Be healthy.
Eat dessert first.
Don't get mad, get funny.
See movies.
Learn new skills.
Read-read-read.
Ask questions.
Listen.
Get a good night's sleep.
Return phone calls.
Make or break your own rules.
Smile.
Dress like a skinny girl.
Walk with confidence.
Wow! Let's go, girls!

It's National
"I'm Glad I Have a Sister" Month

Okay, well, there really isn't a month like this yet, but there needs to be! Just about twenty minutes ago, I hung up the phone after talking with my sister for, oh, I don't know, about twenty minutes. We can talk about anything and nothing. We can talk every day for a week straight, then not at all for a few days because we get so busy and then talk again every day for a week straight.

My sister, Staci, is three years and nine months younger than me. The four-year age difference really mattered when she was eight and I was twelve. We were three years apart in school. Now, well, we are of the same generation, so neither of us thinks about the difference in our ages.

Often, much to Staci's delight, I tell people that I am the younger sister. At first, she was indignant; now she just laughs. My sister is the one person in the world who knows exactly who and what I am and doesn't care. She knows that I love *Sex and the City* and can watch reruns for months on end. She knows that if we go out to lunch, I am either completely into my "healthy food lifestyle" (I hate the word diet) or will pig out with chocolate. She knows all my secrets (I did indeed love John Travolta as "Vinny Barbarino" in *Welcome Back Kotter*).

My sister pretty much knows all about my life and I about hers, yet we never, ever divulge any secrets to anyone else. We are friendly with each other's friends. She handles all the hard stuff with our mother, and I handled all the yukky stuff with our father. The system works for us.

My sister is the one that I run everything by, because she is *the* nicest person in the entire world. I have said this before and I continue to say it: She is just really nice. People like her. Where I am opinionated, my sister stays neutral. Where I might fly off the handle (who, me?), my sister stays calm. Whenever I may be holding a grudge, my sister encourages me to let it go. Where I want to know everything, go everywhere, and meet everyone, my sister is content to tag along for the fun. And she does.

I have a great time with my girlfriends, I really do, but I have the *most* fun with my sister. We have our own shorthand: I never have to completely explain myself to my sister, ever. Sisters sort of allow and encourage this.

Last summer, my mom took my sister and me to New York City for a week of Broadway shows, yummy food, and enough walking for a lifetime. I was in charge of finding the fun, my sister was in charge of getting us there (she is exceptionally good with a map), and my mom was in charge of paying for everything–a great deal for all three of us. My mom made sure we got to the shows on time, I made sure we didn't miss anything, and Staci, well, she directed us wherever we needed to go.

We had the greatest week. We loved the shows and meeting the actors and dancers afterward (my idea). We loved walking through the different neighborhoods and seriously eating whenever and whatever we wanted. Though I directed our activities each day, the one thing my sister thought would be really fun (but that I just could *not* see myself doing) was to take the "Sex and the City Tour." It ended up being three of the most hilarious hours of our lives.

Often, my sister and I try to catch up by doing something together. Over the years, our activities have changed as we grew older. For many years, when we had disposable income, we shopped together. Now we see movies. We also get our kids together whenever practical. Three of them are the same age and the youngest (Staci's goddaughter) goes along with the big kids. They always have a good time together. Her kids love the freedom of my house ("The kids? They're outside playing.") and my kids love the "anything goes" of her house ("The kids? They're watching TV /playing a video game/ playing wii") yet it works. It seems great that all four of these kids can feel comfortable in either house with either set of parents and with each other.

I know I don't tell her often enough how much I truly appreciate her. I love my girlfriends and feel incredibly fortunate to have them, but I would be lost without this sister of mine. How blessed am I to have had the opportunity to be *her* sister. Staci, Happy National "I'm Glad I Have a Sister" month!

Tour de Forest Park

About ten years ago, my friend Sheri, whom I've known since seventh grade, asked me if I wanted to come biking one summer morning with her group of bike riding/teacher friends. Sheri and her buddies have ridden weekly throughout their summer breaks for the last twenty years.

They rarely invite anyone else. Needless to say, I felt privileged, nervous, honored and scared out of my mind. So of course, I jumped at the chance to ride with her.

"We're serious, though. We really ride," she cautioned.

I have always loved to ride and was a bit nervous. What if I couldn't keep up? What if I was the last rider? Couldn't breathe? Couldn't hold a conversation? What if I was just a big drag on their amazing biking outing?

It was a hot morning and after I dropped my kids at camp, I met Sheri and her group at Creve Coeur Park, where we indeed engaged in some serious riding. I was able to keep up, but just barely.

After this ride, I was excited and wanted to continue riding. I described my experience to anyone who would listen, and two of my friends agreed to try it. My friend Susan had a bike and my friend Jenny actually went out and bought a bike.

That first year every Monday morning Susan, Jenny and I rode the bike trail at Creve Coeur Lake. One week, Susan had something to do and missed our outing. We didn't know it at the time; however, that was the beginning of a blissful ten-year biking relationship between Jenny and me. We haven't stopped riding since. Every now and then, someone joins us for a while, but it's been Jenny and me for ten years. And yes, Jenny will tell you that even though we laugh about *Sex and the City* or the crazy antics of our children, I often use the bike outings as therapy sessions. Jenny is a great listener, one of those nonjudgmental friends who honestly, in her heart, wants the absolute best for you. As she puts it, "I just want you to be happy."

What makes me happy is riding with Jenny on Monday mornings, rain or shine. Well, not true. We ride in the freezing cold months of winter, but not in the rain. One cold January morning, after making it twice around the park, we looked at each other and together said, "My feet are frozen!"

Through all the cold St. Louis winters, kids' schedules, and a few injuries, we've kept Mondays as our biking time. There was a back injury and a summer job that sidelined us for a little while, and Jenny has broken a finger twice. However, for the most part, if it's Monday, we ride.

Late last spring, we decided to forego Creve Coeur Park and ride those amazing trails in Forest Park, a gorgeous park in the middle of St. Louis. We had ridden it once or twice in the past; this time, we were really aiming to challenge ourselves. And we did. Forest Park's six-mile trail offers gradual inclines, steep hills and other riders to navigate around. Not to mention the horrible humidity of St. Louis summers. We are able to ride the long hard trail twice and still hold a conversation.

I guess that, in a way, the entire riding experience has offered us challenges. First, there's the challenge of actually saying each and every week, "All right, we are going *out* there and we are going to ride." Each Sunday night we touch base and keep our fingers crossed that everyone's kids are well enough to go to either school or camp on Mondays. We try to keep Monday mornings clear of work, meetings and other responsibilities.

I am not sure whether Jenny and I know the kinds of muscles we have built with our riding. We definitely have gotten pretty strong.

I wish we could say our legs looked like Lance Armstrong's, but suffice it to say we look a little more like Sheryl Crow, which is okay by us.

We are both team riders. We ebb and flow according to who is setting the pace. Sometimes she does, sometimes I do. We also challenge one another. On those Monday mornings when someone is too tired, the other rider gently encourages her with shouts of "Let's get riding, girlfriend!"

Any of my girlfriends will attest that the lure of Forest Park is not just the trails and the interesting sights. It is in fact, Kaldi's Coffee Shop, located just off the park down a side street. Kaldi's is my favorite place to have coffee and hang out with my friends and family. My friend Patti first introduced me to Kaldi's when Joe was born fifteen years ago, and the magic has not faded for me. Talk about a homey place that begs you to pull up a chair with a book or a good friend! In my mind, there is just nothing better.

For me with the need for speed and wind, nothing compares to getting out there on my bike with the wind in my hair, letting my bike just go when I reach one of those hills and flying as fast as I can next to one of my best girlfriends. I am living *in* that moment.

Day Trip

On any given day, there are a million things I could be doing as CEO, President and Laundry Fairy of my household. That goes for all of my friends as well. We are busy people, making sure everyone else has clean socks, healthy lunches and signed permission slips–not to mention keeping up with the slew of papers that come across our counters every single day.

So it was with much pleasure that my friends Jenny, Karen and I planned a day long bike trip. The date was changed a million times due to unplanned weather, meetings and other events we couldn't foresee. But we persevered. We kept e-mailing in earnest, trying to find a day that we could all put life on hold, go biking and enjoy the day together.

On a beautiful day in late September, we finally loaded up our bicycles, gear and Jenny's new puppy, Bailey and headed out to Defiance and Augusta for a day-long bike ride. Though it took us months to plan, the day zoomed by. Finally, all the variables lined up and here we were.

Jenny rented a bike and a carrier in Defiance. I had thought that bringing Bailey along was a crazy idea. (I found out later that Jenny had had some of the same doubts during a very busy week, but decided to go for it. I'm glad she did.)

As I watched Jenny simply load the puppy in the car and later into the carrier, I realized that I had friends who, when they put their mind to something, made things happen.

We began our ride in Defiance at the Katy Bike Rental with the Augusta Brewery as our planned goal. Karen and I had no idea how far it was, but the morning was cool and overcast, perfect for riding, and even more perfect to spend the day together. I had not been on the Katy Trail in years and the gravel was not as bumpy as I'd remembered. We easily pedaled the eight or so miles, chatting, catching up and laughing. We exchanged stories about our kids and our lives, asked a million questions of one another and laughed a lot. Bailey alternated between looking out of her carrier and lounging.

We had a yummy lunch at Augusta Brewery, overlooking beautiful fall scenery. Over lunch, we talked and laughed some more and then got back on our bikes to head the eight miles back.

This day trip simply felt indulgent—more indulgent and decadent than the occasional movie we manage and the lunches we meet up for. We could have spent our day doing a zillion other things: meetings, volunteering in classrooms, grocery shopping, cleaning. Instead, we chose to take a day for ourselves and found that the world didn't stop just because we did.

What a great idea it was. The day was relaxing, inspiring and some of the best *fun* I've had in a while. Later, I thought to myself, "How often can I say that my day was...*fun*?!" (Seriously, searching out fresh vegetables can be fun...sometimes.)

When we arrived home from our biking excursion, nobody was the wiser. Karen made it for afternoon pickup, Jenny made it for carpool, and here I was, bright and happy as my kids got off the bus. As Jenny and Karen drove away, I asked myself, "Why don't we do this more often?" (Oh, yes, the fresh vegetables, laundry, meetings and errands...)

Karen later e-mailed, "My husband, Howard, commented that these women really make you feel good...and you both do!" Isn't that what life is *all about*? I smiled, because Karen and Jenny are amazing women to know and spend time with. They make me feel good about me, too.

Day trips are a vacation in the middle of real life. After that I felt ready for anything—errands, committees, homework....even laundry.

Girl Power

Last March, I received a phone call from my friend Jodi. "I loved your article about volunteering! What a great idea. Why do we have to wait until our girls are 13 to start?" Now, anyone fortunate enough to know Jodi will know that this quick question was followed by a million ideas. Because with Jodi, you simply take a deep breath and hang on. Jodi gets things *done*.

"We don't have to wait," I answered.

"Great, let's do it now."

"Okay. You want to start a volunteer organization for girls who are Samantha and Jessie's age?" I had a feeling I knew where this was going.

"Yes, right now. I always think I want to volunteer and get out of my comfort zone, but it's easier to do in a group. How can we do it?"

Strength in numbers. If we could gather moms and their daughters in a small group, we could pool our resources. Giving back and reaching out is a personal quest that can easily be accomplished in a group setting. Since everyone knows someone who knows someone, we could really reach out past our small group, not to mention having a great time while doing it.

After a little more brainstorming, I contacted Linda Rosen and Susan Hobbs, friends who have navigated their way through the volunteer world. They both agreed to help us in whatever way they could (and to this day, continue to do so). Shortly after the phone call, Jodi and I met with Susan Hobbs at the Bread Company one sunny Tuesday and Girl Power was born.

While Girl Power is meant to be a fun, comfortable, community-oriented group, we also wanted to teach the girls exactly what it means to give back. We wanted to take them places where their energies could be well used and appreciated. Ultimately, we wanted to empower our girls to feel like they could make a difference—whether it was serving dinner at a shelter or packing boxes at a food bank. We wanted to make volunteering a part of their young lives so that it would become a natural way of life.

While we both felt completely committed, we knew that we wanted a group of people who would feel good about this commitment of time and energy. So we set out to organize other moms with daughters who were nine and ten years old and who shared our goal.

The response was astounding. We had no idea other people felt the way we did and we couldn't wait to get started. It was as if this group was just waiting to happen.

I invited Bob Manges, a volunteer from the Ronald McDonald House to our first meeting to talk about volunteering and the organization he worked for so passionately. While the girls got to know each other through games and ice cream, the moms brainstormed ideas.

On August 16, we held our very first Girl Power sponsored lemonade stand and made over $400 for the Ronald McDonald House. In October, we brought dinner for the ladies at St. Patrick's Shelter downtown. At each and every event, the girls and moms come through with flying colors, always willing to do more, stretch themselves and learn about other people's circumstances.

Jodi and I talk and e-mail daily. Other moms have taken on leadership roles within the group, which was also part of the plan. Our current goal is to perform community service long-term and to be role models for the girls. While we are doing the leading now, our hope is that, by the time the girls are 13, they will be leading us.

Both Jodi and I took a deep breath and held on. You never know where a good idea might come from and blossom into something even more rewarding for everyone involved.

We are making a difference…one child at a time.

The Playgroup Moms

Almost everyone I know has one. Some friends even have two. Ask any mom you know about a playgroup and you will hear a version of the following: "They are my best friends." Or, "We still get together." And the best, "I wouldn't have survived without them." Most playgroups are formed for a baby's or child's socialization. However, those moms who have a really amazing playgroup know that sometimes the playgroup ends up being just for them.

Our playgroup is celebrating its fifteenth anniversary. We met when we were all sleep deprived, questioning our sanity, and dreading Daylight Savings Time. And to think it all started because six intelligent, ambitious women decided to have babies.

We met when we carried our newborn babes in arms into a weekly early childhood class. We had burning questions about eating, sleeping and general well-being. Oh, and yes, we had questions about our babies.

Our instructor was a mild-mannered, knowledgeable, kind and open-hearted woman by the name of Lynda, who promised us all that we would indeed sleep again. Not soon, but we would.

Those first few classes, we talked about sleep deprivation quite a bit. None of us could believe how tired we were. Although feeding and bottles and doctor's visits were part of the discussion, we almost always circled back to sleep. Lynda was kind and offered many strategies to try and save our sanity. Joe's favorite part was the end of class when we all sang songs together. My favorite part: the other moms. They saved my sanity more than once!

I clearly remember feeling like a mom for the first time one

October day when baby Joe and I made it to class. I still wasn't sleeping, still hadn't lost any baby weight, and was deep into post-partum depression. But that day, I remember feeling like a mom. Some weeks, the only time I got out of my house was to Baby Class. Sometimes, the entire day was spent with that goal in mind.

Our class at the early childhood center lasted until the holidays. When that ended, we decided to keep the group going by meeting at one another's homes. This was an outdoorsy group, so when the weather got warmer, we congregated at various parks around the city.

Sometime during that first winter, we decided to go out to dinner. No babies. No husbands. No worries. We have been meeting once a month ever since. It has been one of our best decisions.

We have never gone to the same place twice. It was a highlight and a major accomplishment to get ourselves out of our houses, showered and dressed each month for our dinner. Along with the humorous stories of school and babysitters and a tremendous amount of laughter, there was always chocolate.

To be honest, I would not have survived my kids' early childhood without the women of my playgroup. Initially, they knew me only as a parent, sleep deprived and wearing Kenny's shirts (you don't even want to know about that). I didn't get back into my own clothes until Joe was 10 months old, at which point someone commented, "You're a tiny girl! We thought you were just small with huge boobs."

One of the most enjoyable aspects of playgroup remains the differing opinions, outlooks and experiences that everyone brings to our group. Though we were all at the same starting place, having had babies within weeks of one another, everyone's previous experiences were interesting. Some of us didn't let anything bother us, and others were concerned about everything. It helps to talk all these things through with other moms that I really trust.

When the kids were still young, our playgroup decided to add fathers twice a year. We have had family picnics in the spring, holiday dinners in the winter, and once or twice we all met to swim. We have even had holiday parties when we hired a chef so that everyone could enjoy themselves.

My kids have brought me so many wonderful experiences. I am privileged to say, one of the best is the playgroup moms. Our playgroup is a fellowship of like-minded moms who have become loyal friends. It's hard to imagine that Anne, Janet, Sally, Penny, Michelle and I have been talking kids and life for fifteen years. Thanks for being such a big part of my world….all these years later.

Old Friends

A few years ago, I received this e-mail:

"Is this the same Pam Wilson that I might know?" it began. The e-mail continued, "It's Cutlan!!! How are you, girl?"

I smiled, because when you are in the presence of Cathy Cutlan, you have no choice but to smile...and smile wide. Cutlan (as she was known throughout her youth and continues to be referred to this way) is a woman filled with sunshine and fun, life and laughter. If there was ever anyone you could describe as being her true self, it would be Cutlan.

In fact, Cathy and I have known each other since kindergarten. We went to the same elementary school until third grade, when I moved. When I moved back in seventh grade, Cathy was at a neighboring middle school. Everyone knew everyone, so I knew "about" her from afar. In high school, Cathy's school and mine were rivals (in the friendliest sense), and we both marched on drill team. (Hers was much more precise than ours and won many awards.)

Then, in college, just when I needed a burst of sunshine, who shows up second semester freshman year on my dorm floor? Yes, Cathy Cutlan. We reestablished our friendship quickly and solidly. She was tons of fun, and I am smiling as I remember our adventures that semester. We encouraged everyone to tan with us between classes, using foil reflectors and baby oil. We stayed up late, dancing in our dorm rooms and somehow involving most of the floor. We even "borrowed" fraternitys' composites and displayed them in our ninth-floor front windows, wondering why campus police would come to rescue them. Cathy's roommate, Rosie, helped me pass Spanish that semester. I'm not sure when we had time to study.

There are aspects of Cathy's personality that everyone knows and loves and that make her who she is. For one, she knows exactly what she wants and makes no secret about it. When we recently got together, she reminded me, "I wanted a real college experience. Fraternities, sororities, classes, dorm life. But I always knew what was waiting for me at home and what I really wanted." And I knew she was right. At a time in my life when I had no idea about a longer-term plan, Cathy had already formulated one for herself. The great part about it, though, was that she was willing to really "have" the college experience. She lived in every moment, later saying "I totally remember that great time back at MU–great memories!"

What *I* remember most about that time is the innocent fun we had; the good, clean, honest fun. Cathy simply sees the fun in everything and makes any and every situation worthwhile.

On the first night of our sophomore year, we went to a party at Phi Kappa Psi, and I accidentally bumped into a young man I had known about in high school. His brother had been a student teacher when I was a junior (the Police song "Don't Stand So Close to Me" was most likely written with him in mind). I knew who this guy was and we talked well into the night. Cathy was there as I fell head-over-heels in love for the very first time. That semester, Cathy and I pledged different sororities (if I could go back in time and change anything, it would be this decision) and I struggled to keep my grades up while dating this new guy and continuing to have fun with Cathy.

I managed two of the three, bringing my grades up the next semester. Cathy went home at semester to her boyfriend, Kenton, who later became her husband. I was even in the wedding. Cathy has raised two amazing boys and has stayed happily married to Kenton to this day. She has kept up with all her friends, seeking out many on Facebook.

Cathy stays optimistic whenever she can; she would much rather stay focused on what is good and happy. However, like the good friend she is, she will honestly tell you about rougher times she's been through and what she decided to do with the experience. She will unwaveringly give you her honest opinion about anything you tell her. I was having a hard time allowing myself the freedom to not stay friends with women whose daughters had been unkind toward my own 12-year-old. Cathy looked at me and said, "Why would you be friends with them?"

Every now and then, we get together, and this year was no different. I e-mailed Cathy late one night after accidentally coming across photos from college, including the college sweetheart I haven't talked to in years. "Do you think I could find him?" I asked. That started a flurry of e-mails that led us to a three-hour lunch one Monday. The minute I saw her I started smiling and I didn't stop the entire day. We chatted and caught up and I felt the shift within our friendship. We are nearing 50; this has changed our perspective on keeping up with friends, making time for the important people and thinking about how we want our lives to look like from this point on. Luckily, Cathy still knows exactly what she wants.

Whenever I think of Cutlan and our friendship, I know how very lucky I am to be enveloped in this woman's warm glow. She e-mailed me later that day, "I LOVE how some things never change! You were such a 'bright' part of those years for me, so I am glad to have the 'bright' back in my life!!" I may not have reconnected with my college sweetheart, but wow, did I ever get lucky to stay connected with Cutlan. She may tell me I'm the brightness, but I know without a shadow of a doubt that Cutlan continues to bring sunshine wherever she goes.

Surviving Suburbia

I sent the following e-mail out to all of my girlfriends hoping for some interesting answers. Many of my friends wanted to talk about it with me…and many more than I thought chose not to answer. Sometimes when I asked someone directly they answered and in a few cases people were happy that I asked and even happier to answer.

This was the request:

Hi!

I am working on a project and would like to know your **SECRET of surviving suburbia**. The hope is that the project gets published…but I can't promise anything. You can remain anonymous if you want or you can let me know that you want your name used.

This project is very near and dear to my heart and that is why I chose the people (YOU) I did to contribute. I have big plans for all of these secrets….

Also, please keep this to yourself. I know it would be fun to send it to your three best friends, but I really need to know the people for this part. Actually I would love to get as many answers from as many women in suburbia as I can…maybe for the next project. Once I know for sure about publication, I will let you know and we can shout it from our suburban roof-tops!

If you don't want to contribute, that's okay, too. I'll still love you and consider you one of my people.

If you do want to contribute, please send me your secret (it can be funny, comical, serious, something your mom told you, something your college room-mate said, anything you want-ok…NO pictures of cute men!) by Friday, March 18th to this e-mail.

Thank you more than you can know-

What I received back was amazing insight:

Diane Friedman

Thank you for thinking that I survive suburbia!!!!!   I have to think about this but I will get back to you. I really have been thinking about this while I have been packing up my kitchen. I think my biggest secret to surviving suburbia is ORGANIZATION. I have a really good calendar that is my bible for the entire family. I try and have all activities, birthdays, etc. etc. on it. Everyone knows that they must consult with the calendar before making plans. I couldn't survive without it.

Michelle Wexler

I don't think of myself as surviving "Suburbia;" it's "Parenthood" that I've survived–so far. Here are a few key things that have helped me. 1. I never pass up an opportunity to listen when my kids feel like talking–even if it's midnight on a school night and I'm dead tired. For some reason, both of my kids have found the "witching hour" to be their most comfortable time to unload. 2. Remembering what it was like to be their age–the good, the bad and particularly the fun. It has allowed me to empathize with my kids when they've hit a rough patch, and it has helped me to let go when they have pushed for more independence. 3. Instilling in my children the knowledge that, even though I trust them, I worry about them and I can't help it. I think they do their best to let me know where they are and when they'll be home. 4. Finding one or two parents who carry the same level of worry as I do, or who are even a bit more neurotic about their child's safety and whereabouts. I always knew that if I couldn't reach my daughter by phone or text, her best friend's mom would know exactly where they were–usually at the friend's house that had no cell reception in the basement. 5. Never revealing my outside sources to my children. Whether I learn something that amuses me or concerns me, I'm never willing to risk having a good source of valuable information dry up. I think it's good that kids know we parents talk. They just don't need to know who said what.

Cheryl Adelstein

I survived Surburbia by leaving it. I'm a proud city dweller, which definitely has issues relating to public education. I hope what my children have missed out on in terms of academics and amenities, they are making up in life skills, dealing with diversity and learning what it's like to be a minority.

Cara Bauer

A few secrets: Sit on my front porch when the weather is nice to see what is happening on my street. Frequenting restaurants which are actually in the City of St. Louis every once in a while. Heading out to the country to smell cow manure (1st generation off the farm, the whole dirt thing is thick in my blood). I garden, it is my religion. Not many people seem to garden anymore, they don't know what they're doing. I need to be in the dirt otherwise I go insane.

Anne Pokoski

I don't live in the suburbs; I live in an inner-ring suburb, which is a completely different thing.

Carla Scissors

By moving to the central west end! Altho its no secret... Your royal dancing subject Cheers. Carla ps unless suburia is a state of mind... no mini van no matter how many sports we do!

Staci Pruitt

My couch at the end of a long week!!!

Surviving Suburbia
Cindy Held Tarshish

It was easy when we were first married, with no children, zipping around town in my Mazda RX7 complete with stick shift; I would never own a mini-van! There, I said it, no matter how many children I had, how deep into the suburbs I lived, no matter how many carpools I had to join, I would never, ever, own a mini-van.

Three children later the temptation was there. With three sons to drive to religious school, play dates, and every team sport you can imagine, the "luxury" of that Astro mini-van was almost too hard to resist. Those doors that magically slid open at a button's touch, the VCR movies to quiet the crowd, the extra cargo room for my Costco runs–but no, I would not cave, I would not be like every other suburban Mom in the pickup line at Hebrew school, I would hold strong.

My husband took up the cause as well; buying me every type of SUV until we hit the jackpot with my extra long Suburban; ironically named after the place I was trying to escape. I was the envy of the cul-de-sac, every Mom wanted to ride up high like me, superior over those with their shiny new vans. Then it hit, my world spiraled downward, the gas crisis of the 90's. My gas guzzling best friend had to go. I survived and even learned to enjoy my Honda Pilot, still clinging to the notion that I would never park a mini-van in my driveway.

Now I wonder if it was worth it; two of my sons are adults with their own cars and the third just got his permit. Sure, it was entertaining to teach them to parallel park a Suburban, but did I really prove something? Darn right I did–you can see by my driver's license that I live in the heart of suburbia, but my car will never give me away!

Cindy Dreifke
Pam, What can I say, but stay true to your friends, they will always be there for you...Always be open to new friends because you never know who you will meet...Soccer, football, hockey, baseball, dance and cheerleading friends may come and go, but your true friends will be there when the tough times come..I wish I had known this

advice when my kids were younger. It was the good friends that were there when I needed them the most...I haven't seen those that I thought were friends after my kids left the sport...

Hi, Groovychickpw! Robin Marrah

I've been thinking about your email and contemplating. I'm wondering how you are even defining suburbia and whether it has negative or positive connotations. However, here are my reactions to your questions. Maybe they fit, maybe they don't. If it's published for profit, I want my fair share. Ha ha! Here are my thoughts:

Find a really good friend or two or three with whom you can: Co-op in any way (childcare, grocery or general merchandise shopping, carpool, sharing dinners, errand running, sharing recipes), Show up anywhere with no makeup, comfy clothes, and possibly running late and just enjoy each other's company, you can ask and share secrets on raising children, balancing and surviving family issues whether it's marriage, children, or extended family, balancing work and family, confiding mistakes and resolutions. Just stay connected with work friends, former work friends and personal life friends

With your family: Cook meals together, Order in and play games or play music, but NO SCREENS and don't answer door or phone, Snuggle and watch TV together, Work on art even if it's play-doh, a coloring book and crayons or paint-by-numbers, Volunteer for charitable purposes.

With your spouse: Have dates at home or out, alone or with other couples, Set and work on goals together.

When alone, indulge sometimes: Spend the day in your pajamas reading or watching TV or a movie, Go to a movie by yourself in the middle of the day, Get outside and walk, garden, explore the area, Stay in your pajamas all day and just clean and organize, Work on something to spoil a friend, your spouse, or your friends, Volunteer outside of school.

Karen Sher

The first thing that comes to mind is "The secret of surviving suburbia is a great street to run on with a Starbucks at the finish". And of course… "What is said on Wydown stays on Wydown!"

Mindy Grossman

Okay - secrets to suriving suburbia - don't get caught up in the gossip, find "true" friends that have the same beliefs and values that you do, and as often, as possible, get out of the suburbs!!

Lisa Massa

I don't think I have a secret to surviving but do think my job keeps me sane. Work gives me a safe outlet for my competitive nature (versus how my kids did on their latest tests or in the art fair or track) as well as just plain wears me out so I look forward to going home and relaxing in my little slice of suburbia.

Jodi Schneiderman

I'm not sure how to answer this, because I was born and raised here and I always wanted to be here. At different stages of my life different things were important for me and to me. Before it was all about my kids and my business. Now, it's more grown up like going out dancing with my girlfriends. My family has always been important in my life through every stage and always will… especially my mom who is an amazing person. What's exciting right now is that as my kids get older and more independent, my husband and I are in a new stage-trying and finding time to spend together.

Aida Greenberg

Look up as much as possible instead of down? Meditate on trees, the taller and older the better? Smell the flowers, not the garbage? For me it's get a way AWAY (no pun intended) to get back to nature. Blade as much as possible on trails, count to three so you don't give the bird to the person who just stole the parking spot you'd been waiting for for five minutes (jk)!, and smell the earth when you garden.

Nancy Greer

I have lived in a number of places - suburban, urban, international, rural. each place has been different in many respects. my needs/ desires have changed with each place. i think i adapt as a course of nature. i have come to think that we survive/thrive because of what is inside of ourselves. each "chapter" of my life has been different and while some chapters have been easier, each has been uniquely giving. if we allow ourselves to get stuck on a certain "diet" of culture, surroundings, even people, we won't sense the gifts of the present. i honestly think what it boils down to is my capacity to just embrace where i am right now. i honestly do not think i could ever be bored. each place, stage offers me time to discover something new or maybe just time to do some things that i want to do. i have found that the more "out of my box" places have been my sweetest opportunities. they usually aren't places i've "stayed", but then, i have never really ever "stayed" anywhere!

i am very much trying to focus on embracing rather than surviving.

Kim Bolourtchi

My secret is simple- find something you love to do that takes you out of the daily grind at least once a week. For me, this is dance. I firmly believe that we each need at least one hobby that is uniquely ours, where we can immerse ourselves and forget about the world if even for a brief time.

Jean Knittel

There is no such thing as a perfect child or a perfect parent. Nothing and no one is perfect. You have this child and I have mine. You are this kind of parent and this is what kind of parent I am.

The days are long but the weeks are short. Treasure this time because it goes so fast!!

If I were writing a book I would elaborate on There is no such thing as a perfect child or a perfect parent. Nothing and no one is perfect. You have this child and I have mine. You are this kind of parent and this is what kind of parent I am. Maybe I would explain in more detail things like it doesn't really matter the exact age when a child reads as long as they start reading. Parents feel as if they did something wrong when children the same age as theirs do things before their own child does. It is bad for both the parent and the child. Our society has so much information now that we have too many things to measure our selves against. If I had Lisa Keithly's gift for words I would elaborate in much greater detail. We are what we are and so are our children. The sooner we make peace with that the happy we will all be.

Karen Wasserman
Getting away from the chaos and taking my dog and going for a walk in the park to enjoy the outdoors and beautiful scenery!

Carrie Wallach
I think my secret to surviving suburbia is just trying to stay grounded in God's word--to not become too absorbed in our extravagant world. I'm not sure if that's something you'd be able to print, or would even want to, but it's the truth. I try to remember that it's all because of Him and I try to keep that in my heart. I'll never get it perfect, but I do try to walk with Him and love others as He does. It's hard, but worth the effort.

Karen Kessler
Not sweating the small stuff, saving the emotional energy to get through the big stuff. And knowing you will get through it.

Happiness is an emotion not a state of being. It comes and goes from day to day. Finding contentment is where it's at.

CPSIA information can be obtained at www.ICGtesting.com
Printed in the USA
LVOW120810291011

252641LV00001B/4/P